Leadership Challenged

A Middle Management Memoir

By
Christy Claxton

Edited by Nicole Drilling

Copyright 2024 - Christy Claxton
Txu 2-453-188
First Edition
No parts of this book may be duplicated without consent

Acknowledgements

I want to extend my heartfelt thanks to the people who believed in me as a writer. My wife, Tammy Johnson, thank you for always encouraging me to "just write." Nicole Drilling, your gentle suggestions are a model of great leadership. You pushed me to write my whole truth. Samantha Cruz Johnstone, thank you for being a blunt copy editor. I always know I can count on you for the truth. Although I'm singling you out, I want to thank my entire team at Ziff Davis. Working side by side with you for so many years taught me so much about commitment and leaning into the talent around me. You are so much more than a work family. You still make me laugh and think and care every day.

Title Page	1
Acknowledgements	2
Prologue	4
Chapter 1 Working it Out	5
Chapter 2 The Stories That Make Us	10
Chapter 3 The Enchilada in a Burger Joint	21
Chapter 4 The Human Experience is the Greatest Teacher	36
Chapter 5 Work and Music in a Small Town	47
Chapter 6 The Peace from the Porch Project	70
A Brief Interlude	82
Chapter 7 The Trees Are Tired	86
Chapter 8 Work Ethic was a Career Killer	95
Chapter 9 It's Like a Bad Marriage	110
Another Brief Interlude	113
Chapter 10 Don't Expect People to Share Your Dreams	115
Chapter 11 Tectonic Shifts	121
A Final Interlude	125
Chapter 12 Practical Leadership Tips from the Middle	126
Hiring	127
Training	131
Career Development	134
Mentorship is Leadership	137
Passing the Baton:	139
Epilogue	141

Prologue

This is a book about leading from the bottom to the middle. It is not about the C-suite; although it wouldn't hurt most executives to read it.
It is also a middle manager's memoir.
If you're looking for a self-help or "how to" business book, this isn't it.
If you believe growth lives within creativity, you might find this helpful.

Chapter 1
Working it Out

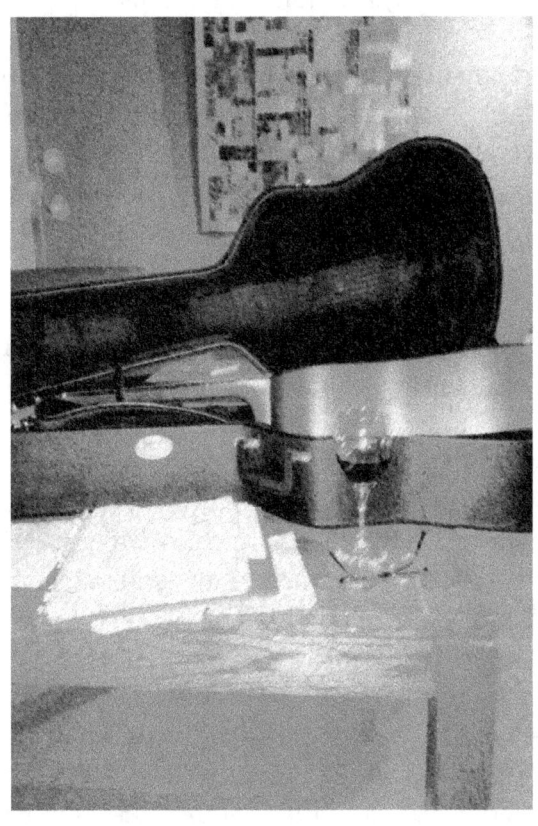

I got laid off in May of 2024. I think all of us that were affected were still either reeling from it, desperately grasping for something new or coming to grips with our weird sense of relief. Whatever we went through, I know that every former workmate I talked to had the same underlying theme. Authenticity.

I would say that my state of mind was a slow, slow reeling that required constant calming, coupled with an amazing sense of freedom. What I lacked was patience. I wanted immediate outcomes. I move very, very fast. Slowing down would be a huge asset. Y'all. I am trying!

Maybe you all can relate. Maybe some of you shove it down into your deepest psyche in order to get up and do a job every day. What am I talking about? Creativity. Uniqueness. Bold thinking.

Why do we think we have to hide that? What is it about today's work world that makes us believe we're in a cog that only grinds when we conform? And here's the crazy part. Companies advertise disruption, creative thinking, exciting new ideas, fast paced excitement, blah blah blah.

Here's the problem with all of that.
An idea is only as good as its execution.
I've seen a number of executive level leaders throw spaghetti at the wall only to burn out the teams that have to clean that mess up.
That's not groundbreaking. It's not creative. It IS disruptive, but only in the pejorative sense.
It made me realize that Imposter Syndrome goes both ways.

Whoa!! Did I just suggest white men are imposters?

I did.

I think we can all agree that there are people in senior and executive positions who aren't qualified to be there. I was told that senior level jobs are offered on the golf course. Relationships outweigh qualifications. Sounds like I won't be advancing my operations career via job boards, but if I'm a good enough "bullshitter," I may have a chance. There are those who are convinced they are leadership material when they really aren't. I think those of us who are suffering a collective work exhaustion are now or have recently been exposed to poor leadership.

Leadership is not spreadsheets, presentations and schmoozing.

The very first principal of leadership is simple:

Never Forget Where You Came From

Period.

Honestly, the janitor may be a better leader than a CEO.

How do I know this? Personal experience.
Why was I more drawn to the cleaning woman than my boss?

She was more authentic. She looked me in the eye. She smiled and said hello when she saw me. She listened. She seemed to have time for me.
I realize that executive leaders are short on time and that they are juggling big responsibilities, but if you make it that far in your career, at least learn the illusion of time. You have one minute. If you engage with your team by using eye contact, standing still, and participating in active listening, that one minute will seem much longer to your employee.

We were all the new person once. We all had those horrible early job experiences where we felt abused, dumb, frazzled and directionless. My first job as a manager offered the lovely perk of nightly hard cries from my living room couch. A hopeless sense of stress and degradation. No real support, but plenty of accusations and yelling. Even a little harassment that bordered on quid pro quo. Because I was young, I just thought that was how a job was supposed to be. That somehow, that emotional beating would move me right up the ladder of success. It didn't. I had to quit to save my own soul. And that meant starting over in a similar situation, and so forth. It was age that pulled me out of that cycle. Life experience. And I never, ever forgot where I came from. No one deserves to feel that way just to get a paycheck.

I have become a fantastic leader of people. A motivator. A shit umbrella. A gateway. A servant leader. I was never afraid to learn my team's jobs and help out. I could pull a poor performer back from the brink because I was really good at understanding what got them there in the first place. I wasn't interested in just my own skin. I believed in people, and I saw them as individuals. And I never thought I was perfect or beyond growth.

I got out of their way and encouraged them to make their ideas work. And almost always, the ideas were a success.

Now, here I am. Working it out. What's next for me? Honestly? I am not technical. I can learn stuff and do it, but it doesn't excite me.

I'm a creator. I'm a people champion.

I get such a deep sense of accomplishment when I see a young worker excel, grow, promote and succeed.

I also get a deep sense of accomplishment when I can use my creative mind and spirit to help those in at risk situations step up to something better. Oftentimes, it's these people that are the brightest future for humanity. If they remember where they came from, then they will be the compassion and strength we're going to need to evolve beyond a keyboard and monitor.

So, I have aged over the last 12 - 15 years. Not just chronologically, but physically and emotionally. I tried hard. I kept my integrity, and I championed a smart and wonderful team of operations experts. And I put up with a lot of stress and unwarranted crap. I feel proud of my accomplishments; even if I'm an older version of myself.

Now it's time to take that experience and make it a better path for those who come after me.

I once had an elderly gentleman say to me,
"My dear. We're like horse shit. We've been all over the road."

Chapter 2
The Stories That Make Us

I signed off at 5pm on a Friday and bid farewell to my small-town listeners. The little radio station had scratched an itch I wasn't brave enough to pursue. Music. I am a musician. A songwriter mostly. But now it was time to pack up my belongings and head to College Station for graduate school.

School was what I needed. After an unsuccessful attempt at fulfilling unrealistic dreams that I was somehow leadership material at the age of 22, with an English degree from Texas A&M, was about as naive as it gets. Nobody told me that the diploma was not a red-carpet entry into adulthood. After a few weeks of desperate job hunting for something that paid more than minimum wage, I sold my old car and bought a one-way ticket to Los Angeles. My California transportation was a bicycle. My job was a low paying gig at a beachwear shop. My life was work, home, typewriter. I was lonely. I lasted 6 months.

A trip back to Texas for a visit reminded me that I need to see the stars. I rolled down the window of my friend Michael's car and smelled dirt from the fields. We had Stevie Nicks cranked up as loud as we could get her. I knew I belonged back home in Texas. My boss in California was kind. She advanced me my last paycheck and offered to ship my things home on the company UPS account.

I stepped off the plane in Austin, in August, and nearly fainted from the Texas heat and humidity. But I was home. Literally. I moved in with my parents. I was 23 years old and living at home. In 1988 that was not a normal occurrence. Kids moved out and grew up. But I was home. I took a job at the local radio station, and for $800 a month, I played old country music, read obituaries, and joked on air with the locals. I actually miss that little job. However, I was so young and driven to be somebody; and by "somebody" I meant money and success. My youthful self was not mature enough to see the value of a small-town radio experience. I didn't see the success of being the center of small-town life. The voice of the community.

As a chronically curious person when it came to other people's life challenges, I picked up a story off the AP wire about a woman who was arrested for trading her daughter for crack. Back in those days, the AP wire was an analog printer that spit out little snippets of stories throughout the day. I was tasked with finding the ones most relevant to my listening audience and mixing them in with the local news. This story was exclusively for me. I tore it off the printed page and kept it. It would become my Master's thesis. My impetus for heading back to A&M for an advanced degree in creative writing - something that was new to the graduate English curriculum. So off I went to become a writer and professor. In my mind, a professor was the ultimate social climb to success and acceptance.

The English department at A&M had no idea what to do with creative writing students when the degree was launched, so I earned a Masters in English with a creative writing specialty. I wasn't graded or judged on my fiction or plays. I was judged on a critical introduction that I was tasked with writing to introduce the creative meat of my thesis. To this day, I think that introduction was requested so the professors on my advisory committee would have something to do that they understood. It was unusual to me since none of them had a problem critiquing the master works.

The education became secondary to my two years in that master's program. In those two years, I planted the foundation of who I am today.

I grew up.

Trust is a core principle in life. So is love and friendship. And sandwiched between these two extremely important learnings for life, I was blossoming into a creative communicator. Be it songs, short stories, or my bold and socially explosive play that I wrote from that little snippet off the AP wire, I was finding my voice. In those two years, I finally grew up and away from the small-town kid that bumbled off to the University at the age of 18. Life was coming for me in ways I was yet to understand.

I began to write fiction about the real life around me. Whether it was my life or someone I observed, I produced a mad burst of stories. Today I can read those stories and see myself working it out. Becoming me. Therefore, I'll insert creative passages and some of my short fiction into this book because I think it's necessary for anyone who thinks outside of the garden variety leadership model to massage the creative side of their brain.

I took a playwriting class my first year of graduate school. It was taught by a Pulitzer winning black man who was a storyteller through and through. Charles Gordone was the kind of man you never forget because he wove his fictional truth into your bones. On the first day of class, he spent lecture time telling us a crazy story about his childhood where two jealous brothers took him into the woods and cut off his soft curls. Their hair was "nappy." (I can still hear the way he emphasized that word). When their mother found out what had happened, she whipped the two brothers because she adored Charles' soft curls that made her baby more desirable in a white world.

After the story, Charles said, "read the chapter on premise and then come to class with the premise for a play." The class was silent. My friend timidly raised his hand and asked, "Can you explain what you mean? What is premise?"

Charles shouted, "Boy! You get an F for today's lesson."

The premise was in his story, but could we decipher it? It could be a couple of things, in my mind. It could be "jealousy leads to punishment," or "racism leads to appropriation" or "soft curls on a black child led to an identity crisis" (due to an expectation to act white). If I could master this single lesson on human behavior and its consequences, I could master leadership. Charles' story was a lesson in paying deep attention to the world and the people around me and understanding what motivates them to take the kinds of actions that they do.

What drives people? What drives society? What drives a workplace? Whatever that is becomes a premise for real life.

In the meantime, I was creating my own premise. I was in the throes of my own identity crisis. I was finally maturing enough to understand that I wasn't a small town tomgirl looking for an intelligent and kind husband. I was gay. I was a lesbian from a right swinging small Texas town. I was terrified. But my own emotional hiding was starting to suffocate me, and I knew I was about to write out my truth in the form of short stories. These stories would edge on emotional brutality and satire. They would start to crack the surface of my stand against bigotry, xenophobia, elitism.

Let's start with a story….

Ice

He took his coffee black. Laurie kept it filled to the brim, a glass of water on the side. Every day he came and sat at the same table. No one ever joined him, and he never greeted any passersby. He walked through the door with slow, deliberate steps, paused briefly, then went to his table. Laurie always made sure the table was unoccupied by 2:00 P.M. She never greeted him; just took the cup of coffee and glass of water to his table. He never looked directly at her. He looked through and past her, and she always had the impulse to either glance over her shoulder or feel her face to see if there was a hole in it. She didn't even know his name.

He had eyes like blue ice. Sometimes, if Laurie stared at them long enough, they turned white and fiery. She imagined them to be like angry young stars, so cold they would burn, blazing through the black universe. His face was pale, which only intensified the eyes. Laurie had noticed a few lines around them, but it was impossible to tell if they were there because of age or worry. She couldn't believe they were the result of laughter. The lines' ambiguity made it impossible for her to tell how old he was. There were no other tell-tale signs, and no matter how hard she tried to study his face, her focus always drifted back to his eyes. Laurie stood fidgeting at the bar, letting him burn through her into the wine rack behind her.

She never saw him eat anything, yet he wasn't thin or unhealthy. If he would only wave to her and ask for something to eat, she could hear his voice. She couldn't remember what it sounded like because it had been over a year since he first came into the cafe. He had said, "Coffee black and a glass of water," without looking at her.

She could remember the words but not the voice. She tried to put a voice with the eyes, but there was no match. Laurie thought of that first day when she had been busy stocking the bar. She turned around to get some glasses and was startled to find him staring. His gaze was so intense that she pulled her hands up to her mouth. Then she realized he wasn't staring at her but through her. She noticed how magnificent his eyes were, and she found herself staring into them with childlike fascination. She had never seen eyes like that. She waited for his gaze to shift so that she could go and fill his coffee cup. Then she would be brave and tell him that he had beautiful eyes. Suddenly he blinked and dropped his head. He placed a few dollars on the table and left. Laurie was so startled by the abruptness of his action that she forgot to call, "Thank you and come back!"

He did come back. Every day for a year he had been walking through the swinging French doors at 2:00 P.M. He paused, walked to his table, and as he sat in the same chair, facing the bar, Laurie placed his coffee and water in front of him. For a month she tried to speak to him but always stopped her voice just before it passed over her lips. Somehow, she knew the sound would bother him. Maybe even make him angry. If waiting for him to arrive at 2:00 P.M., coffee in hand, made him happy, then that was what she would do. She was satisfied just to feel his stare as she watched him from behind the bar. Sometimes she closed her eyes and felt his burning gaze. It touched her like fingers, and she let it move across her body, hot and slow. The eyes moved closer until she was face to face with him. The hot fingers encircled her waist and drew her in. She began to melt with the heat as his lips touched hers with the same intensity as his gaze. She always had to open her eyes at this point because she was afraid of going any further. His stare never changed, but she wondered if he could see what she was thinking. She thought he could. She believed in a silent union between them. Laurie always stood in the same place because it was her way of giving to him. There was something about standing there and letting him burn through her that was more fulfilling than anything or anyone else in her life.

Her entire adult life had been surrounded with loud, bragging men who strutted and brawled to impress her. Then they took her to bed only to forget she was there. They stared at the headboard with wide eyes and drowned in their own sensations. When it was over, they either turned over and snored drunkenly or sat up and pulled on their pants and mumbled a "see ya later" as they closed the door behind them. Either way, Laurie's only comfort was to curl into a ball under the covers and hide her loneliness. She lay there in a realm of semi-consciousness. She heard every sound and felt every movement. She woke up exhausted, and if there was a man in her bed, she wouldn't speak to him. She walked into the bathroom, feeling the icy tile on the soles of her feet, stepped into the cool air of the shower and turned on the water and let it run down her aching chest and tense stomach. She pressed her hands against the shower wall to keep them from shaking and cried. No one ever recognized the tears as anything but hot shower water running down her face. If a lover was there, he usually stumbled in and peed while she cried silently. He flushed, causing the shower to scorch Laurie's skin, stumbled out and was gone. Laurie wiped his yellow droplets off the toilet as she dried off. She had never even talked to a gentleman except to take his order, and most of them tried to be clever and flirtatious. No one was ever lonely.

Laurie refocused her attention on the ice blue eyes. She glanced at his hand as he lifted the coffee cup to his lips. There were no rings on his fingers. She thought he must be alone and impossible to be with. It was appropriate that he was surrounded by three empty chairs and the sounds of echoing laughter and chatter spilling from the corners of the cafe, bouncing off the cement floor and over his steadfast gaze. He lowered the coffee cup onto its saucer and reached for the ice water. As she quietly poured, she heard him crunch on a piece of ice. She looked up, and he was staring directly into her eyes. Not through them but into them. She was so startled, she splashed coffee into his saucer. Her stomach felt like a scream, and all her senses fell into it. She could feel her eyes become circles, and she opened her mouth to speak but only gasped.

"Don't look away," something inside of her whispered.

His jaw tensed, and the anger in his eyes sharpened before he jerked his head around and stared out the window into the blue gray sky.

She took a chance.

"Such a gray day, isn't it?"

"Yes." It was only a whisper. She couldn't even see his lips move.

She felt warm tears well up behind her eyes. She turned and ran to safety behind the bar. When he finally turned back to his normal gaze, through her and into the wine rack, she felt disappointed. She had missed her chance. Laurie was too far away to tell for sure, but she imagined the whites of his eyes to be pink from hidden tears. She was sure the irises were bluer than she had ever seen them. She continued to watch. Slowly the eyes began to pale until they were ice blue and then almost white.

Each of us carries secrets we're not ready to share. We carry pain, shame, heartache, failure, stress, danger, illness, and defeat. We are socialized to hide that away, most definitely in the work world. And for a good reason. Brokenness can break an organization. Just one unresolved issue that is allowed to manifest in the workplace, the home, a hangout, a church, can fester into a wound that eats up every objective, goal and bottom line an organization strives to uphold.

A compassionate leader would recognize the signs of emotional disruption and address it. It's certainly not the boss' job to get involved in personal matters, but it is a good leader who can find the right way to redirect and heal the damage to an organization. Just because emotions are not a data point doesn't mean they don't exist to negatively affect the workplace. Believe it when a team member complains about unwanted behavior from a workmate. And I don't mean just sexual behavior. I mean anti-social behavior that may manifest as non-responsiveness, gossip, personal complaints, disruption of other workers' time, etc.

There's a premise. Find it and manage it. But before that can be done, everyone must check their biases. We all have them, and if we allow them to drive decisions, there's no turning back from failure. If not soon, then certainly later, biases catch up with an organization.

ICE is about quiet pain and how that can manifest as fantasy. If we begin to believe the fantasy, we never grow.

Here's an exercise you can try.

Write a one paragraph story or summary of a story for these premises.

1. Non-communication leads to negative assumptions.

2. Opinions lead to termination.

3. Kindness leads to victory.

4. Myths lead to spiritual suicide.

5. Glass Ceilings lead to broken necks and opened minds.

I'd like to carry on with my own story based on the last premise.

Chapter 3
The Enchilada in a Burger Joint

In the early 1990's Texas A&M was barely emerging from its conservative, and some would say, narrow-minded reputation. Women still struggled, minorities seemed to exist at the graduate level, but not as much in the general student population, and LGBTQ+ was completely unaccepted. Back then, it was LGB. Binary in its definition, although most of us under the label called "bisexual" a gateway identity to lesbian or gay. Yep. Even our own community was binary. Humanity was a broad spectrum, but most of the colors were undetectable to the human eye at that time.

I struggled with my own identity throughout the fall of my first semester of graduate school. I spent my afternoons at the gym with Michael. He was proudly out and actively defining himself as a gay man. His boyfriend was something of a suspicious emotional trainwreck with a murky past, and I was naive to the world I was finally starting to accept.

"Ice" was a story I created to better understand my own inner workings. Because I wasn't ready to announce my own sexual orientation, I created a heterosexual main character. But the setting was my favorite restaurant. It was a bistro that had good energy and good coffee. I could spend my mornings there eating baguettes and drinking black coffee as I worked on my short stories and budding play. I had my setting, and I had my own personal premise.
Although we'd only met a few times, my future girlfriend worked there. She had the most crystal blue eyes I'd ever seen. They were shockingly bright and intense. So I could weave the setting, myself and Wendy into a story with a premise that went something like this: Self denial leads to emotional emptiness. I needed to get brave and come out.

Wendy had a twin, and we became friends as we moved through the same social circles. A circle of closeted young people who stuck together, but had ways of covering their truth. For the lesbians at A&M, we always had the willing straight man or gay cowboy who would masquerade as our boyfriend when it was time to protect our identity from family. The early 90s were not a time of family acceptance, and many of my friends had horror stories about coming out to their parents. I knew I wouldn't have that problem because my mother was and still is defiantly liberal, but I was afraid of me. Of a future I couldn't clearly see or understand.

Wendy's sister met me at a party that Michael was throwing. It was a dinner party drenched in booze and dance hall music. We decided to play the Telephone Book Game. Before the internet and smartphones, thick paperback books were distributed to households. They contained every person's and every business's phone number, plus advertisements. Depending on the size of the town, those books could get very thick. We played the game with Dallas phone books. They were about 3 inches thick and because of the cheap, thin nature of the pages inside the book, they were wobbly and unstable if you stood on one. The game was almost impossible.

A team of two had to stand on a telephone book, and their feet could never leave it. Four quarters were placed on each side of the book, on the floor. The team had to pick up all four quarters without falling off the book. If anyone fell off, that team had to take a drink (usually beer, but we played with vodka). If no one fell off, another book was added until eventually, somebody would fall off.

My teammate was Michael's boyfriend. We were good. We had balance. We made it to about 5 or 6 books before we fell. That doesn't mean we weren't slamming vodka. In fact, we were drunk and still managed to stay on that stack of books. By the time the game was over, I was so drunk that I told Michael I had to go home. I was feeling my emotions bubble up along with my dinner.

In a fuzzy memory, I am standing at my car with him and someone I didn't really know - a cowboy named Gene. I threw up and as I wretched, I cried and told Michael I was gay. As most friends do, Michael responded, "Oh, honey. Everybody knows that."

The next thing I remember is waking up in my own bed, undressed and clean. I called Michael and asked what happened. He said I came out. Gene drove me and my car home, and he followed. He then threw me over his shoulder and carried me up to my apartment where he undressed me, cleaned me up and put me to bed.

Damn.

That is loyalty and friendship. And a very powerful lesson in trust. Ask yourself. If you take the proverbial fall from grace, is there anyone there to pick you up and support you? Do you feel safe to show any vulnerability? If not, would a little burst of compassion improve your workplace and productivity? Truly, I believe without hesitation that loyalty is something every organization needs, but it has to be earned; even in the messiest situations.

I never feared for my life, but I sure didn't provoke a reason to be afraid either. My friend circle was very liberal. It was my family away from family. I began playing folk music with my friend Stacy at a local live music joint. We also hosted a Tuesday night open mic that exploded into an alternative scene that lived itself out in a very open and public way. The owners of the club were liberal rabble rousers. They loved the scene we created.

It was surprising how quickly Stacy and I built a following. At that time in music history, singer/songwriters were on the rise. Indigo Girls had broken through the masculine barrier to become more than a lesbian folk duo. Stacy was a crazy fan and loved to sing Indigo Girl covers. I did not want that comparison. Regardless, crushing on a lesbian duo made for big turnouts. Honestly, we didn't understand our power. We were shocked by "come ons" and requests for our phone numbers.

From the stage, I could look across that room and feel a bit of terror. It was bawdy and loud and free. And sitting at a table right in front of the stage was the electric blue-eyed woman. Wendy. She tuned out the noise and fiercely focused on the music. It took me a while to approach her, but when I finally did, it was messy and weird and self-forgiving. She was my biggest fan. She was my book buddy as we thrilled over great literature. And I was actually paying for grad school making money at that little club.

The scene became more broadly known, and we attracted all walks of life to that Tuesday night event. We were breaking through the old guard. It doesn't mean we eliminated bigotry, it just seemed we were allowing even the most middle of the road students to flex their individuality. It was good.

During those years, I lived with Wendy and my friend Michael in a duplex that had once been WWII military housing. The place had no AC and only one wall heater. It was a dump. We paid $225 a month for it because it was considered graduate student housing. We called it the graduate student ghetto. We were all poor in that little neighborhood. We were a neighborhood of mixed-race couples, Chinese political refugees (Tiananmen Square was only a few years in the past), elderly people who lived below the radar, and students just as poor as us. If someone on the block qualified for food stamps, we all ate well because empathy was high among us. Everyone deserves a balanced, home cooked meal from the government. My household ate plenty of beans and potatoes. They arrived in a display of disapproval from my mother who thought we were squandering our opportunities.

She was right to a certain extent. That old wartime duplex hosted boozy, jam-packed parties that roamed the place like heavy smoke from too many cigarettes. I never knew everyone who showed up for our late-night revelry, but everyone was welcome. We played gay dancehall music the old-fashioned way - vinyl spinning under the direction of Michael. He was a connoisseur of esoteric tunes: all backed by the iconic beat of what he called the "whip machine." In between records, we'd take turns singing songs or maybe even listening to the rag tag folk rock band Stacy and I created. It was loud. It was a love fest. It was stoned and drunk and secretive. It was well worth the disapproval of my mother because it was the education that I needed at that time in my life.

As it became more and more evident to me that my hard scrabble attempt at graduate school was nothing more than the bragging rights of a master's degree. I let go of any notion of becoming a professor and focused on becoming the creative I really was. I was sustained by beans, rice, beer and cigarettes, and I was nurtured by songs, and for the first time in my life, an understanding of what it really meant to be in love - to love someone in a way that I knew would be forever. I walked through the final year of grad school writing a play that no one would ever produce on a stage, and I created some very intentionally bullshit critical introduction to it while wearing hand-me-down Levis and macramé sandals. And I felt good and loved in the dream of something greater than academia.

Even so, I knew that I was a natural born teacher. I wasn't writing to entertain. I was writing to wake up the reader to something they could change if they felt moved to do so. Bigotry, stereotyping, social assumptions, assimilation, religious brutality wrapped around the cross. I wanted to make a difference by moving people through characters they weren't supposed to care about. I instinctively knew that telling stories was the best way to teach. It engaged the student, and it had the potential to create an investment in positive social change. So, I partied. I sang. I made pretty good money with my songwriting partner and soon to be lifelong close friend. We were making good noise that even got us noticed by the legendary Texas Governor, Ann Richards', campaign team. We sang our hearts out at her political rally. We shouted into that echo chamber and felt like we mattered as every marginalized Texan's favorite gubernatorial candidate listened to us. Standing in a ballroom in a hotel in Dallas, playing our protest songs that railed against the Reagan Administration was one hell of an ego boost.

Stacy is a showtunes kind of woman. She can belt out Broadway hits spontaneously. So, when Carol Channing and Liz Carpenter walked over to us, it was one of the best ego boosts two college students could ever imagine. They locked arms and listened to our songs with delight. They praised us and thanked us for our music and our message, and they walked away. A few minutes later they returned with Ann. Now we're talking about the kind of pride that can burst your chest open.

Carol said, "Play the ballad of the GOP for Ann. Ann, you have to hear this." The name of the song is "Mind of the Madness." It's a dark folk song about greed's way of forgetting humanity, but Ms. Channing gave it her own title. We played, and Ann Richards was delighted. She enthusiastically thanked us, and we went back to College Station on a cloud. I still have the thank you letter she wrote to us. And looking back, I can see that it was one of the first times that we were part of change for the people. I just wasn't able to seize it as an opportunity to lead my milieu towards activism yet. I was still grappling with myself and growing up.

We were at our favorite folk club the night Ann Richards won the Texas governorship. When we announced her victory, the walls vibrated with joy. I was infected with the rewards of doing good work.

For those looking in from outside of College Station, the question was always, "why are you there instead of The University of Texas?" I would reply, "Every burger joint needs an enchilada."

I think that's important even in corporate America. Diversity does matter. Allowing some of the culture of a diverse workplace to seep into the company culture is important. The blinders that protect affinity bias can be the very thing that destroys a successful mission. Disruption is not just some over privileged young man, who mistakes himself for a demigod, throwing wrenches into traditional industries with the hope of extreme success. Disruption from within the organization can be powerful if the right kind of leadership is in place.

Leadership has to see it, identify it, and nurture it. To expect young workers to see it in themselves is too much to ask of them. No one on Ann Richards' campaign team reached out to Stacy and me and asked us to join them. Had they done that, our lives would be very different today. I only speak for myself, but at 24 years old, I was ripe for mentorship. I didn't have it. I had a thesis advisor who could only feel her own skin and fashion some assignments for a dry critical introduction to my creativity. Nobody said, "You're different in a way that would benefit academia."

I most recently worked for a worldwide company that threw spaghetti at the marketing wall, waiting for something to stick. Its Hispanic Employee Resource Group presented a well-researched piece on the multi-billion dollar power of the Hispanic dollar. I had been asked to join this group as an ally. I worked with a few of the group's leaders to present the kind of research and information I knew would resonate with senior leadership. Mostly, the CEO. No spaghetti, but a well-researched, data backed presentation that laid a path towards a new and powerful revenue stream. After a ceremonial pat on the back, the research was ignored. Pursuit of that market was never encouraged, and when employees did work on an action plan, it was relegated to "extracurricular." Companies that have understood this demographic and marketed in a way that directly speaks to the culture become merchants of choice for a very loyal demographic. But that takes vision and an acceptance of a level of disruption from within; especially if it's proven to be a good bet. I think that sometimes the bar graph on the daily markets acts as jailhouse guards to leaders who simply can't believe they might be in their own way. For me, it was a flashback to my graduate school days, sitting in my thesis advisor's office and focusing on her expression of disapproval. A dismissal of my hard work. We didn't have a name for that feeling at that time. Today, we call it Imposter Syndrome. It stabs you right after you present good work to the person you most need approval from. Then it grows like a cancer that is very, very hard to cut out of your psyche. My logical mind knew I had done great work, so I did my best to let defiance take a swing at that unwelcome imposter.

In late 1991, as I was wrapping up my classroom studies at A&M, and getting ready to move to Austin, I had a small inkling of how powerful disruption could be, and how powerful me and my marginalized friends could be if we were allowed to grow up outside of societal traffic signs. All of us grew in different ways. Some were able to hold onto the free-spirited way of life that defined our time together in that old duplex, but not me. I fell right into line and let my true self and my dream career go. The imposter won.

I had a job at a one-hour eyeglass company that I had gotten through a friend. I fell right into the hard work, do everything right specimen of an employee that I had been raised to be. I was seen as a future leader in the retail business. Nothing about that job was remotely like who I was as a creative, but I knew that I couldn't move to Austin without some kind of job, so I took a little promotion to help open new stores in Austin. I took on my new responsibilities for $5.75 an hour. I was finishing the critical introduction to my thesis, and I could see no other way to get out of College Station. Wendy and I made the move.

We rented a tiny house just east of I-35 and south of 38th1/2 street. We struggled financially, but we jumped into the music scene and the art house film theaters, and the hiking trails and we felt at home. But only for a little while. Everyday pulled me further and further in line with societal expectations of me. I was slowly giving up. She started a teaching career, and I became angry at myself and the world around me. We didn't make it. I went off to become a store manager and then an area manager for the eyeglass company. She drifted back to the hippy scene of our A&M days. We never spoke.

I became accustomed to long days, hard won success, and the constant verbal abuse and fear mongering of poor leadership. It was a male driven ethos that measured success by personal bonuses, womanizing, and showing off. On the other hand, it was the typical female driven HR department trying to introduce less touching, more conservative dress, a corporate lexicon, and a knockout job of simply not seeing the poison.

I went through a series of bosses. Finally, a woman was in charge, but the men who came before her warned me that she was "a bitch." They tried to scare me into not trusting her. They wanted me to be afraid. They wanted to believe that I was going to miss them once I answered to her. It wasn't like that. She taught me two very important leadership lessons that became core principles in my own growth. Here they are:

1. If you can get your job done in 4 hours, and you can produce outstanding results, it's ok to leave. Go do something you enjoy.
2. The two drink rule - as a leader it's important that you are accessible to your employees. If they like you, they may invite you to one of their happy hours. Don't say, "no" because if you do, you just lost their trust in you. You have sent the signal that you are better than they are. Go. If you only have one drink, you may be seen as disingenuous - there to check the "cool boss" box. It's ok to have a second drink. Then you're human. You're accessible, and you'll gain their trust and loyalty. But if you drink that third drink, you're doomed. You've lost control and if you're getting drunk, you've lost their respect. It's a balance. Always be the leader, but not the drinking buddy or the disconnected boss behind the office door.

Where I could immediately act on #2, I never mastered #1. There are a couple of reasons why. First, retail doesn't work that way if you're a good leader. You stay and help. You make yourself available. You don't walk out on your team. I'm glad I was that kind of leader. Not only did I support the team, I learned their jobs. Therefore, I deeply understood my business. The second reason is buried in the first reason. Retail industry or not, I simply invested way more than I really needed to. I wore myself out because I suffered from Imposter Syndrome and immaturity in the workplace. I wasn't even 30, so I was certain I wasn't worthy of a day off. Or even a shortened day. I drank that Kool Aid until I couldn't. Here's what happened…

I never got over the heartbreak of the breakup with Wendy. She was a first-class athlete who also read constantly, and she and I shared that love of literature, film and good music. She was shy, gentle and kind. She was, to me, what love feels like. I could feel her presence at a concert hall. I went to local music events with a nervous sense of how I would react if I saw her. She simply lived in the back of my heart and mind. Even as I dated and committed to short-term attempts at moving on, I could not shake her.

One night, at an event at Waterloo Icehouse, at 6th and Lamar, I ran into one of her friends in the bathroom. I felt uneasy, but the friend was warm and engaging. They expressed such concern for me, and then asked if I had talked to Wendy. I said no as that nervous edge that followed me into music events started to nag at my stomach. The friend smiled, looked directly into my eyes, and said, "You should call her. I think she'd really like to hear from you."

I called the next day and set up a friendly meetup at the Wheatsville Coop Festival happening that Sunday. We sat in the sun and talked and shared book and movie recommendations like no time had ever passed between us. I always thought of Wendy as a bit of a hypochondriac. Today, I recognized that she had a healthy dose of OCD, too. I know that's why I had to check the oven 3 times before going to bed when we were together. So, when she said she had been feeling strange, and not really good, I didn't think much of it. She said she was going to the doctor to figure out why she felt so weird. Honestly, it felt like home. A normal sunny day between us. We left in good spirits and went on with our weeks.

About a week later, I got a call, at work, from her twin sister. The call sat me down hard and took the breath and spirit out of me. "Wendy has a brain tumor."

Within another week or so, she was in surgery to remove it. I was in the process of opening another retail location for the eye care company I worked for. My newest boss was there with the team. We worked late into the night to merchandise the store and set up the point of sales system. While we worked, Wendy prepared for surgery. Her twin told me that she only wanted her family and me in the recovery room. The next day, I was obligated to go back to work and continue the store set up because I didn't dare ask for time off. As the Area Manager, I told myself that I could not do that. I was middle management. I had to be all business and put eyeglasses first. I finally worked up the nerve to ask for one hour off to "go see my friend who just had brain surgery." My new boss begrudgingly allowed me to do it, but she reminded me that this store was my responsibility, and that I should be putting it first.

Let me stop right here and say this. If you work somewhere that expects you to put a for profit retail company before anything else, you're in the wrong workplace. Firstly, this boss assumed my team was a bunch of directionless idiots with no critical thinking skills. She had no trust in them, and probably me either. That's micromanagement. Minimum wage plus commission isn't going to keep anyone around long enough to become an expert in eye care if they're considered too irresponsible to decide where red or brown glasses frames should be displayed.

I headed to the hospital for my visit. It was meaningful, powerful and affirming that this was my person. I should not have felt rushed to spend time with her. When I arrived and walked into her recovery room, she asked her family to leave us alone. Then she looked out the window and said, "I made a terrible mistake." I responded, "Let's not worry about that right now."

We never got back to that moment. Her health deteriorated over the years until she was forced to live with her parents until she died 20 years later. If someone were to ask me what held me prisoner and often kept me from using my power to climb into a senior position, it would be twenty years of waiting. But no one did. No one ever thought someone with my determined and sometimes overbearing personality would have inner workings that sucked the will out of me. That boss waiting for me to return from the hospital most definitely saw nothing but the return of a resource.

I went back to work. I was angry at my boss. I was starting to realize that inhumanity did not make a company successful. I didn't say a word as I walked over to the cash register and continued working. My boss asked in a cheery and completely disingenuous voice, "how's your friend?" I looked her in the eyes and said, "She has cancer." I immediately turned away and went back to work.

I put in my notice about a month later. I was done with stress, tears, and some idea that I should put a company that no longer exists today, ahead of humanity. My own humanity. My last day was unceremonious. I had built up my value in my own head, but that corporation taught me a good lesson.

We're all expendable if a spreadsheet makes the decisions.

Looking back on that time today, I can also see that I had been promoted to middle management without any mentorship or real support. It really wasn't a career growth success story. It was all business. Although I had two women bosses at that job, only one gave me any real growth advice. It was golden advice in the

1990s, but it wasn't going to make me a great leader. Granted, I strongly believe in both of her suggestions, but I was at an age and career stage where I could have used so much more. Instead, I quit. I left as a disillusioned worker who had already forgotten what it felt like to be a creative or use that part of myself to inspire others.

I laid in my hammock and drank iced tea for a month before I went back to work in a lesser position in the same industry. I was in a band that Stacy and I created once we both moved to Austin. That was my creative outlet. It was fun and kept me in a state of hope. I was living the quintessential Austin experience. Hopeful musician, playing clubs for pennies while working a job that would eventually overtake the music.

Three years later I checked out and, and defied that experience. I decided to make my living playing music. It was something close to financial suicide, but it was also a spiritual goldmine. I was seeing the world in a way I had never imagined, and it became a foundational building block of the leader I was yet to become.

Premise: Ignoring identity destroys potential.

Leadership Lesson: Remember the above premise and recognize it as an opportunity to build a strong culture without blinders.

Chapter 4
The Human Experience is the Greatest Teacher

Here's a story...

Run the Fastest

He was frozen there in the starting blocks. Track and field had been his dream. He tried and tried to run the fastest and throw the farthest. He just never went anywhere. An eternal winter had made him stiff and sluggish, but one more attempt at a heroic sprint was all he wanted. He froze on takeoff. He'd been like that for three months. Frozen.

Expectations had always been high for Mark. Disappointment was all he ever delivered. Pretty much, no one really paid attention anymore. No matter how the heat was stacked, he couldn't win it. He had tried performance enhancing drugs, every brand of shoe that ever claimed to make a champion, and even a few totems in his running shorts. Nothing. The harder he tried, the further he fell behind. He was like an engine nobody ever greased. A rusty has-been. Now, here he was, in an eternal crouch, feet pressed against the blocks, fingertips propping him on the track, eyes fixed straight ahead, muscles taught and ready to spring. The air went cold right before the starting gun. His mind had been racing for ninety days. "Now what? What do I do now?" He was beginning to feel dead.

On the ninety-first day, the sun stayed in the sky a little longer. The day was pleasant and mild. Puddles, long frozen, began to thaw. A spring-like light cast its glow across the long jump pit. Since he was so frozen, Mark could even hear the distant roar of the crowd and the balmy scent of suntan lotion. He knew if he could turn his head, he would see runners lounging mid-field, waiting for their turn to sprint. He knew he was holding up the show with his frigid predicament. It was embarrassing, really. Then from his filmy peripheral, he could see a lanky fellow named

John approaching him. John was a 1500-meter runner. And he was good. He kept a steady pace that left him energy to spare for the last 400 meters. He was a track and field standout.

John entered Mark's full field of view, and he stopped, turned and gazed once he was in front of Mark. He slowly cocked his head and studied the situation in front of him. He sighed and looked a little sad. Was that pity? Mark didn't want it if it was. But what could he say? He looked like a statue. He just had to take it. John shook his head and then sat down on the track. He made little swirls on the surface with his index finger. Then he looked up and said,

"You don't get it do you? Mark, you try too hard. Nobody really cares if you win. Truthfully, they don't care if you lose. You've abused yourself in your pursuit of the gold medal to the point that you're making us all suffer eternal winter. It's springtime, and here you are, frozen like an ancient mammoth."

Mark's mind was racing with his usual deflections designed to change the subject. He really needed to blast out of the blocks and show John he could do it at least once. He knew that success was always preceded by many failures, but he never wanted to be one of those guys frozen on the track. Didn't John understand how important this race was to him?

As if John could hear the voice in Mark's head, he said, "Dude. I get it. Just let go of the race and enjoy the run. Can you think about that? The joy of running?"

This ticked Mark off even more, but quite frankly, he was finally willing to listen to someone. John continued, "And you know what? If you don't want to run, then don't. It's O.K. Just let go of it. Besides, your predicament is keeping the rest of us from running. We LIKE to run."

Mark never wanted to get in anyone's way. He just wanted to win. Now here he was, frozen as a failure, and a nuisance to boot. John stood up and walked away. The sunlight lingered. It really was nice. In fact, it was wonderful. Mark imagined himself lounging in center field, waiting to run. He gradually noticed pain in his toes and fingers. He also heard the roar of a crowd. He could hear runners behind him. The sound of footsteps got louder and louder, and then runners entered his field of vision and ran on by. They seemed so relaxed. They looked so free. Mark found himself smiling in his mind. He found himself enjoying the runners. Now he could feel his ears burning and the tiniest drop of water on his neck. He was thawing out! He readied himself to sprint.

The sun rose to the center of the sky, and the ice encasing Mark melted to leave a puddle on the track. He knew he could launch his race, but he didn't. For the first time in months, he stood up and stretched. Without much thought at all he began to walk, then jog. It felt good. Just a steady pace as he trotted around the track. This went on for what seemed like forever, and that was all right. He was really enjoying the run. The crowd came and went, but Mark kept jogging. He ran for all of March and most of April. By May, he was ready to take a break, so he did. He went to the center of the field and laid on his back. He closed his eyes and napped.

On June first, the announcer called the line-up for the final heat of the championship sprint. Mark heard his name called. He sat up and looked around. Did he really want to run a race? No. He did enjoy running, but that was all he needed. With that in mind, he got up and strolled to his lane. He crouched in the blocks, and when the gun signaled the start, he effortlessly sprang out of the blocks and just ran for the sake of running. When he crossed the finish line, he didn't even know he had won the race. After he received his medal at the end of the track meet, he walked home wondering where he would put the thing. For the first time in his life, he noticed a field of wildflowers. He had walked this route a hundred times, and he had never noticed the flowers. Without much thought, he took off the medal and threw it into the field. It barely gleamed in the sunlight because the lush colors of red, purple, blue and yellow surrounded it, but the effect was nice. Mark smiled and breathed in the spring air. The chill was finally gone.

I spent way too much money to make a solo album, but it was exquisite. I was excited to travel the country promoting it by singing my songs to new, and in my mind, devoted audiences. The feeling of freedom and adventure was exhilarating. I'd always worked hard for very little money, so this was no different except that I was in control.

Step one was finding someone to rent my little house in South Austin. I agreed to rent it to a single mom who was a "private dancer." She was ridiculously flush in cash, so I never had to worry about her not paying her rent. She was honest. She was doing her best to raise her toddler daughter in a good way. But her generic name was probably fake, and I doubted her dancing was a hands off career.

As we'd come in and out of Austin, from the road, we always stopped by because there was always something to repair at the house. It was becoming clear that my renter was probably not mentally stable. The house was taking a beating. And occasionally a minor issue would be turned into a disaster only to have us arrive to be asked to babysit. We would sit on the bus and watch children's movies until the wee hours. When my renter returned, I would stay up late and talk to her. She satisfied the storyteller in me. She had a premise. Uncovering it felt invasive.

She was bright and articulate, and as she talked, I learned she was running from a fundamentalist family in California. Something told me there was a level of brutality that caused her to take an anonymous journey to Texas only to dance for men as a way to survive. I was also getting a lesson in judgment. On the surface, this was not someone I would ever include in my friend circle, but as I took time to get to know her, I found there was no reason to assume her job made her less intelligent, less sensitive, or less determined. She was in a space in her life where the survival of her and her daughter was a fierce priority. Was her judgment sound? Not when it came to men. She allowed her romantic relationships to dissolve into abuse; much like I suspect her upbringing had been. And with that, I could see her mental health unravel. It manifested physically into the deterioration of my house's interior. I knew I would never move back into it. It was full of too many recent demons. When the year of touring was over, the house would have to go.

An older, more experienced me would have been a mentor or at least a resource to help this young woman make the transition into the stable life she wanted but had no idea how to achieve. What the experience of knowing her did for me was start the ball rolling in my empathetic and passionate psyche - that place where wrongs deserved to be righted. It was a spark that could drive my songwriting while it ignited an ember that would become my hallmark as a leader and socially active community builder.

I want to stop here and offer this bit of advice to future leaders. Community building is not just for nonprofits and social movements. It belongs in the workplace. It's not the same thing as company culture. It's something much deeper that may start in a single department or among a group of company peers, and if leadership sees that what's happening is positive, it's time to step out of the way and let the community grow into an asset for success.

In chapter 1, I suggested that executive leaders learn how to make one minute of engaged listening feel like much longer. If a leader is really paying attention, they'll pick up on the swell of "community" that might be developing within the company. Leaders need to join and be genuine as soon as possible. First, it gives them the opportunity to keep the community positive, and secondly, it will become a source of inspiration that can create new and exciting ideas.

The Black Lives Matter movement launched Diversity, Equity, and Inclusion initiatives in many companies. By 2024, we know that most organizations tooting the DEI horn were not genuine. And even worse, not brave enough to stand up to their own fear of change. They fell for the easy way out, "it's the way it's always been done." Regional politics took over, and the pendulum started to swing low again. There's no long term good that can come from this. Companies have agreed to jump back into an echo chamber. Social innovation will bypass them. Disruption is ripe in this atmosphere.

I truly believe that community creates purpose. That purpose might be supporting the relationships of people you've come to care about in the workplace, and in my experience, the community that was my team didn't leave. Even in the most challenging times, the team stayed together for each other, and the company benefited from a reliable operations team with deep institutional knowledge. Until new management engaged in mass layoffs, it was a team that leadership trusted and understood could manage itself with the best outcomes for the company. That team fell apart when the community was gutted by layoffs.

Back to my music days… Musician personalities are some of the hardest to navigate, and that includes my own. We're a sensitive and egotistical demographic. Our insecurities are overwhelming, and we carry the torch of imposter syndrome better than anyone. As I traveled in support of my solo album, I found out very quickly that nobody was nearly as interested in my music as I thought they would be. Outside of national radio airplay, music is regional. I arrived in a new city each night to an audience that had never heard of me. My situation wasn't unique to touring independent artists. What we do is create a community that helps us cross over into each other's regions.

My other resource was the LGBTQ+ community. As a lesbian musician, I could corner a piece of that market. Relationships were my survival. I just had to get people to the show, and I couldn't do that without other musicians. In turn, I owed them an audience in Texas. It turned out that I was better at producing and pitching another artist's show than selling myself, so I eventually went in that direction.

The first six months of touring was simply dumb luck. My girlfriend/manager booked places from Austin to Salem, Massachusetts and we hit the road. I woke up early every day to sit at the front of the bus and watch the world go by. We had calculated that we could sustain this leg of the tour on $45 a day. That would include any money made from gigs and CD sales. We were just getting by and that was ok. By the time we hit Atlanta, I was starting to grow weary. Sleeping in a different place every night was unsettling. Sometimes those overnights were scary. Homeless people would knock on the bus door. Street activity in the middle of the night would keep me awake. So, by the time we got to Atlanta, I was deeply grateful to an older woman that we met at a campground when she offered to let us park the bus at her home for a few weeks.

I still wasn't settled. It was about a month into the tour and the feeling of being disconnected overwhelmed me. We had no friends besides this lady, so if something went wrong, we were on our own. I came as close to a nervous breakdown as I've ever been. Anxiety overwhelmed me. I felt trapped and lost at the same time. Forty-five dollars a day was dangerous, but we carried on.

I was scheduled to play the Millennium March on Washington that was sponsored by the Human Rights Campaign. The march was surreal and empowering; especially as I watched an Episcopal minister get into a shouting match with one of the protesters from the Westboro Baptist Church. Their signs were graphic and gross, and their message of doomsday hate has no logic or place in the country. The crowd was huge. It wrapped me in a blanket of community unlike any I had ever experienced.
I played the festival that followed the march and was introduced to lesbian and gay artists from around the country. At least one would become a good friend. Most were like me. Simply busking for opportunity. If we didn't make much money, at least the experience was memorable and worth it.

We got to Boston and spent a few days visiting the only friends we had before hitting the road. It was nice to see a familiar face, but it wasn't going to give our tour any real boost. At some point, the whole thing became an adventure, and no more than that. I could feel myself not caring as much. We ended the tour in Salem. It felt hostile and foreign, and honestly, the whole tourist industry of that town made me sick. It was built on a history of torture, and I could not shake that energy.

We decided to make a straight run back to Texas, but as we pulled out of Salem, the bus engine began to knock and sputter. We didn't figure bus maintenance into our plan. But we rolled into a parking lot for an auto parts store. When we pulled the casing off the engine, we could see that some bolts in the engine were almost completely unscrewed. We had made a very bumpy drive across the George Washington Bridge in New York, and we figured that shook the bolts loose. A nice guy from the store helped us get everything tightened up and back in running condition. We made it home without incident and spent a few months regrouping for the West Coast part of the tour.

The western part of the tour was where we started to create relationships with performers that we thought we could partner with. Financially, this leg was more profitable, and it felt like we were making the kinds of connections that would help us break out of the regional trap. Unfortunately, people make agreements they are unable to keep, and we spent more time promoting them than any of them spent promoting me. That's how I discovered I had a knack for live event production. I didn't break out into a successful music career, but I did find a piece of personal talent for championing and promoting something I believed in and enjoyed doing.

After a year on the road, it was time to sell the little house in Austin. I knew I wouldn't get the best price because the tenant had done a significant amount of damage to the interior. There were even body slams in the wall that confirmed what I suspected. She was abused. But it was time for me to cut that loose and sell the house so that I could move on. I was ready to live in the country. Selling the Austin house would give me the equity and cash to do that.

My girlfriend and I built a scrappy little cabin on 28 acres in Fayette County, Texas. This little 900 square foot place, with a 30-foot front porch would be the setting that launched me into authenticity. Into my true self.

Premise: Bucking the "norm" leads to the right kind of self-discovery.

Leadership Lesson: At the expense of being redundant, never forget where you came from. I came from a dichotomous world that allowed me to experience corporate bumpers to growth and also a free-spirited world of creativity and the community that allowed me to figure out my own brand of leadership.

Chapter 5
Work and Music in a Small Town

The original cabin, off Bear Creek Road in Fayette County, Texas, wasn't even insulated. In fact, we built it from the ground up with help from my father and step-uncle. We knew nothing about building a house. There was no water or electricity on the 28-acre patch of land that I bought with the equity from the little house in Austin. It was a beautiful piece of a larger ranch. There was about an 8 acre hayfield and the rest was woods. A wet weather creek flowed along the west side. It was a rainy winter.

We started to build in January of 2001. Prior to that, we had a little pond dug along the creek. It filled up on Christmas Day after a hard and long rain. Since the season was so wet, the very first thing we managed to do was get the bus stuck where we thought the cabin should be. Critical thinking was key. If that bus sank like a rock, then a house would eventually do the same. So I set out to find a patch of sandy soil. Something solid that didn't stick to my boots. Fayette County is a mix of black river mud and sand. If I could find hard sand, there would be no need for a foundation. We would square the building site and set the concrete piers.

I found a big patch that would be perfect about 50 yards off the wood line. We got our stakes and string and squared off a 20x30 area. Let me say that there is a reason you should pay attention in geometry. Getting that area square was hard. We had all kinds of parallelograms before we got a rectangle. If a house isn't square within $\frac{1}{8}$ of an inch, the walls will be slanted and no door or window will be installed correctly. Exactness was important. This was a new concept to me as a creative. I was tapping into the left side of my brain and problem solving in a whole new way with mathematical logic.

(Pro Tip for DIY types - if you need a perfectly square area, use the 3,4,5 method. Measure a 3-foot line. That represents one wall. Then measure a 4-foot line at 90 degrees to represent your corner and that adjacent wall. If you measure diagonally, the distance from the 3-foot mark to the 4 foot mark should be 5 feet. Adjust until you have perfect lengths and viola! Your structure will be square. Do this at every 90-degree corner. I know this works because my wife, daughter and I built a fence at our current country property, and it is a perfect rectangle if you view it on Google Earth.)

Before we could start building the cabin, we needed a source of electricity. So, we built a lean-to pole barn in a day and backed a huge propane generator inside. That gave us electricity to run power tools. In the meantime, the well company dug our well. With water and portable energy, we built a cabin off of a drawing I made on graph paper. With plenty of arguments, rain and trial and error, we had a dried in building in six weeks. We had the original structure, a pole barn and a well house, and finally an electric pole. To this day, I'm a handyman or builder's worst nightmare. I know how to build a house. I call out the B.S.

Flexing that part of my brain helped me see problems differently. It also allowed me to see that I could do anything in any industry whether I liked it or not, and as most creatives know, the more you can do besides create, the more options you have when you're forced to find other work.

Once the walls were up and the utilities were in place, we moved in. My mother felt sorry for us, so she gave us insulation. For months, we comfortably existed that way. I paired my music traveling down to Texas. Since we only had a 36-foot RV/Bus when we built the cabin, we had to buy something else for getting around. We purchased an old Chevy dually for $1200. It was banged up and ugly, but it ran. I managed to drive it hundreds of miles to a gig and hundreds of miles back on the same day. We were in a house, but we were still barely surviving on music alone.

My partner got a CDL and started driving a dirt truck to make ends meet, and I drove that old truck to any standing residencies I could book around the area. Most of those gigs were tips only, so between us, we were scraping by.

We continued to work with other touring songwriters to help them get booked in Texas in exchange for their help when I traveled beyond the state to their parts of the country. We'd take a percentage of the performance for our booking and marketing services, and we expected the same when we needed them. Throughout the winter and spring, we hosted many artists in the little cabin. Eventually, we decided the front porch that faced out into a hayfield was a perfect stage.

It was the beginning of an amazing project that would define me as a leader. Not that I was anybody's boss, but I was coming into the realization that I could influence more than my tiny circle with music that is presented with community first. We began Bear Creek Concerts.

The county seat for Fayette County is La Grange, Texas. La Grange is somewhat unique for South Central Texas. It's a town of less than 5,000 people that managed to figure out how to survive when the Department of Transportation built a bypass around it. It was a progressive business community that embraced events that showcased the community. Bear Creek Concerts became one of those events.

With the help of music promoters and performers we befriended, we pulled off a ragtag concert in March of the first year we lived there. One of the musicians was an electrician, so he pulled electrical plugs out onto the porch. I used shop lights with red, yellow, green and white spotlights to create stage lighting. Then we passed out fliers, spread the word, set the stage and had a show. This thing would have never materialized without the founders of an indy Texas music ecommerce site, Lucky Boyd and Jinelle Gibson. Scrappy musicians have a way of finding each other to create magic. It was the principle of helping each other out. We were shocked when 60 people we didn't really know showed up with lawn chairs and drinks for the first concert. Clearly, there was a desire for something unique and entertaining. But like most things, interest waned over the following concerts. People knew we were there, so there was no urgency to come often.

When we thought we should give it up due to low turnout, we were encouraged by city and county leaders to keep trying because it was a good thing. And a good thing indeed! Word spread around the national singer/songwriter community. We invited musicians we'd met, and we vetted those who asked to play. We did 8 concerts a year, March through October. We got ourselves on the national singer/songwriter circuit, and that meant I was inundated with press kits from high quality artists that wanted to play from that cabin's porch.

As the concert series grew, so did the cabin. We added a back room and bath that could serve as a guest quarter. We added a big screen in porch to the end of the cabin and extended the front porch to include it. We kept going and wrapped the porch around the other side of the cabin so that it was accessible from the kitchen. And finally, we added a "fancy outhouse" to the end of that porch. Fancy meant it was equipped with the bottom part of a port-o-let but had a sink with running water that ran into the port-o-let reservoir. We could reach under the cabin and pull a lever that drained it after each show. We saved water, we saved our septic drain field from becoming a muddy bog, and we were able to comfortably support the growing audience for Bear Creek Concerts.

Part of the draw of the series was that we hosted what seemed to become a competitive potluck. People brought food to share that was far beyond chips and dips. They brought their best recipes. We always provided a smoked brisket, and the guests would offer up complimentary dishes and desserts. It was becoming its own community.

This became a big operation that required a massive amount of planning. I would start booking the next season by August and try to have it complete by October so I could announce the line up at the last show of the current season. On the week and day of the concert the cabin and the yard (which was part of the hayfield) had to be mowed and trimmed. The grass along the road needed to be mowed for parking. Stage lights were tested and replaced if needed. We hung tapestries across the porch windows and doors to improve the sound. We set up a canopy for the soundboard. We ran cables and set up speakers and monitors and power amps. We tested everything before sound check and then we tested again. It became a big enough operation that two people couldn't pull it off by themselves.

We had friends that smoked the brisket. Stacy became my sound person, and usually a couple of friends would be part of her team. I placed signage on the county road, set up tiki torches, pulled 8-foot folding tables out of the barn and set them up on the screen porch for the potluck, cleaned the outhouse, answered emails and phone calls, set up an artist merchandising table, and made sure we were ready for the audience by sound check. I then jumped in to help Stacy and eventually stage manage and host the event. I think I became known by musicians as that scrappy producer in

Texas that worked hard, took a break to emcee the show in her dirty shorts and hiking boots, and went back to working hard.

I was also known for my off-the-cuff artist introductions. I made them up as I went, so they were funny, personal and as hyped up as a carnival barker. Years later, while stage managing at the Houston Women's Festival I had a volunteer realize who I was, and she said, "Holy Shit! You're a living legend!" …to which Stacy, who was helping me, ducked away to laugh. Well, there you go. Hard work and showing that you're part of the team DOES matter.

Bear Creek Concerts was considered a House Concert. This is a community of presenters who invite people into their homes to hear a touring singer/songwriter or band. The general rule was that house concert presenters do not take any money for hosting the event. They ask for a suggested donation to pay the musician. It's a modern-day patronage of musicians. No money was being made by me. I was dependent on my own music making. The hard work that we put into every concert was supported by a small team of volunteers. I booked and managed the talent, and I worked to keep the volunteers engaged. My partner helped me with the infrastructure of the event and served as house manager.

Even though we had built a positive reputation as community builders in Fayette County, we were barely hanging on financially. I gave it a last ditch effort to tour the Northwest after we hosted a handful of singer/songwriters from San Francisco and Seattle. Now it was their turn to help me. I boarded a plane in Austin in a torrential thunderstorm before the sun came up one Tuesday morning, and I flew to Seattle.

I stayed with a drummer/percussionist who played with me whenever we were in the same town. We decided we'd do Seattle and the surrounding area as a duo. One of the Seattle musicians from the Texas tour booked three venues. The first one was in a deserted part of Tacoma. There were no cars anywhere, and that was concerning. We played to maybe three people at a free event. If I weren't so determined and faithful to my commitments, I would have flown home the next day. It was clear that I wasn't going to have the same experience in Seattle that we offered in Texas. But one of the three audience members was a radio host from Eugene, Oregon. He invited me to come and play live on his show the next day. I borrowed my friend's car and made the six hour round trip. It was nice, but I didn't have any gigs in Oregon, so it wasn't going to do a whole lot for me since music is regional.

The next gig was in Bellevue, Washington. It was a packed and bustling coffee house, but my host musician didn't want any drums, so my friend sat out. A guitar and drums would not have overwhelmed the room. It was packed and could easily absorb sound, and we were not playing rock n roll from the rotator cuff. It was a passive aggressive move to hide the fact that once again, no money would be made. I started to feel panic creep up. I called my Kentucky musician friend, Kiya Heartwood, the next day to find out who I was dealing with. She apologized that I was going through what I was going through but confirmed I was probably screwed in Seattle. She offered to send me money. I declined because she would have done it, and she struggled to make ends meet, too. I still hold her in the highest esteem, not only because she's one of the best songwriters and guitar players in the indy scene, but because she is real and genuine and kind. Find your Kiya in the world. This part of my story is mirrored in the business world. Broken promises, lack of responsibility and people unwilling to admit they're in over their heads are common occurrences.

Final Seattle show. I had NO expectations. Of course, it was a tiny room in a restaurant with a few people packed in it. There was no room for even a snare drum, and besides, my buddy was too pissed and insulted to come inside anyway. I did my set with a forced smile and polite thanks for all the help and packed my guitar and suitcase for San Francisco.

Seattle was hellish on my partner, too. We thought I would make enough money to pay the mortgage and have a little left over. She was scraping by eating collard greens from the garden. And after the week I just had, my jeans were hanging on my hips. As if it couldn't get worse, the airline wanted to put my collector's item guitar in the belly of the plane. I had to pray it was intact when I landed in San Francisco. It was.

I stayed with another musician that we had hosted from the northwest and her boyfriend. I had her stop by a grocery store and I picked up the most filling and nutritious food I could buy for $5. That included a loaf of bread, peanut butter and a large bunch of greens. That was it. That would be my food until I flew home.

Once again, I was set up with bogus gigs with no pay. I could feel my soul changing inside my hungry body. I could not let anyone else be responsible for my success. The only guarantee was me. I had one gig that I think I booked, so that meant I didn't have a driver. I rented a used car that had to be fifteen years old. I did not care. I can drive a stick shift and the thing ran. I drove to another dark and mostly deserted club for what they called a showcase. I got to play 3 songs, and I don't even know if I said, "Thank you." I just walked off the stage and headed to the bar for a glass of water. The bartender was a trans woman who said, "Honey. You look like you're having a hard time of it. Let me buy you a drink." I accepted and sat there dejected and too tired to hardly think. As I finished my drink, a young man who didn't look old enough to be in a bar offered to buy me another drink. I let him. He said, "I never come here, but you have quite a web presence and I wanted to hear you live."

Another bit of advice. No matter what. Keep your integrity, do your best and believe in yourself because you might be surprised by who's paying attention.

I made it home exhausted, hungry and flat broke. I had never felt so worthless. All I could do is put it behind me and start picking up gigs in Texas to slowly claw back into the black. In the meantime, Bear Creek Concerts still went on.

After that disastrous mini tour to Seattle and San Francisco I knew it was time to get a part time job at the very least.

The covenant that was in place around supporting each other as musicians when we were touring in each other's part of the country didn't always pan out. After putting immense effort into showcasing those songwriters from Seattle and San Francisco successfully through Houston and eventually our own Bear Creek Concert series, it was my turn to play their venues, but it was a lesson in betrayal and learning how to spot an illusion of success from people who really didn't have the resources/venue contacts to pay me back. By the time I got on the flight home from San Francisco, I could barely keep my pants on. I was exhausted from weight loss and survival. My partner had been barely eating, too. We needed to make that loan payment on the Bear Creek Cabin improvements. All those add-ons had to be financed. We did not want to miss a payment.

I got home. I was jaded. But I had learned to spot a disingenuous associate, and my bookings for Bear Creek Concerts and any side events got much more discerning. I also got a job as a temporary receptionist for a small local hospice.

So, what does all of this have to do with leadership? It's not like I was anybody's boss. And that's the point. Leaders don't always sit in the corner office overlooking downtown. Leaders can be anyone. In the case of Bear Creek Concerts, I was becoming a leader in the independent music industry by showcasing personal integrity, excellent communication skills, and a tightly run music production event. It was an operation that eventually became sought after to support festivals and other musical community events. That band of volunteers was good at what we did. No one was told what to do. It was simply my job to inspire.

I got out of people's way and let them do their part the way they thought it should be done. I let them teach me their ways, too. I learned how to smoke a brisket in an offset smoker. I learned how to run high quality sound at a live music event. I learned construction skills. And as my little job turned into a full-time commitment as a volunteer coordinator for that little hospice, I learned about compassion in the workplace.

Y'all everybody dies. Everybody has a story, and one is not more valuable than the other. One decides in their heart whether they are willing to listen.

The first time I was in a hospital room with a patient who was actively dying as his family held vigil, I was terrified. It was a vault into a part of living that most people adamantly refuse to visit until they are forced to. My job was to recruit and manage everyday people as hospice volunteers. Their primary duties would be spending time with the patient. More than anything, patients needed companionship, and families needed respite.

As a storyteller, I began to craft a narrative about compassion and the passionate mission of hospice. As I listened to the stories that nurses shared about suffering, joy, abuse, love, pain, loneliness and existentialism, I became invested in the narrative that I desperately wanted to tell. I wanted to lead people to their higher selves without pitching religion. I wanted to inspire a community to support the least of these. I wanted the anonymous lives of the dying to sit within the community of the actively living. I knew in my deepest psyche that it was a connection that could change any society for the better. It wasn't long before I became the professional and community liaison for that little hospice.

I became respected, relied upon, and known as a committed advocate for those in the most need by not only the medical community, but the people of that little slice of Texas. I did it by honing one skill over all others. Listening. Deeply listening.

This is really where I strayed from the corporate definition of leadership. I operated as a result of people's stories. I thought about business from a human perspective instead of a revenue perspective, and it bit me in the ass about a year later.

The small hospice I worked for was sold to a corporation, and that corporation's primary metric was patient census. Everything we did was measured by the number of patients we had on service. This was gross to me. It was the most inhumane metric I could think of. It lent itself to fraud as people were admitted to hospice before they were actually ready. And from there it was a documentation game to justify their coverage. Sure. More people need hospice than use hospice, but we're talking death, and not everyone is ready to face that.

I tried to put that metric out of my mind and tell the stories to make doctors and families understand why hospice was the best choice for a terminally ill individual. And as you'd expect, more than half of our patients had cancer.

In Chapter One, I said I met a man who said we're like horse shit because we've been all over the road. He was actually a hospice patient. One Friday night, about the time of the sale of our local hospice, I was sitting at the receptionist's desk taking last minute calls, so she could have a day off. It was winter, so it was already dark when a well-dressed elderly gentleman walked into the office and sat down. He took off his bowler hat and placed it on his knee. He held his head high. His beard was perfectly trim and what hair he had left was groomed and white. The elegance dripped off of him. His wool coat was fine and very out of place for a small country town. I finished up my call and greeted him and asked, "How can I help you?"

"I'd like to admit myself to hospice. Do you have a minute?"

I could have easily taken his name and let him know a nurse would call him the next day. I was late for a happy hour with friends. However, I made the decision to invite him to sit at the conference table with me, and I let him tell his story.

He had just been diagnosed with cancer and he had no desire to fight it. He decided he did not want his children to know about it, so he was going to take care of his own end of life care. He was animated and a bit flamboyant. He wanted to tell his story. So we sat there for a few hours. Occasionally the phone would ring and my friends would ask why I was late. I finally had to tell them I wouldn't make it.

This allowed me to give this man my full attention. He was such an unusual character for La Grange, Texas that he most definitely sparked the storyteller in me.

His story was a mostly ordinary life told in a way to make it sound extraordinary. He loved his wife and gushed over her sex appeal and the size of her breasts. He told of his early life as a jazz musician with all the smokey, backlit mystique of a movie. He'd been a catch with his good looks and charm. I could hear a mid-century jazz club soundtrack in my head as he described his life in vivid colors and scenes.

Then he stopped abruptly, and said, "You listen with your eyes."

No one had ever said that to me. In fact, I believed I was a distracted listener that didn't really watch the speaker, but this man was different. He was interesting and at the same time mysterious. So I smiled, and he carried on.

He said he left music to design furniture. He even designed pieces for Madonna. He and his wife and children lived in Chicago, but his wife died of cancer, and her suffering was unbearable for him. He watched as her pain took over without relief, and he felt helpless and devastated. When she died, he was angry at doctors, God and a generally brutal and insensitive world. He moved to La Grange to live with his brother-in-law. We finished our conversation, and I assured him we'd call his doctor for hospice orders on Monday. He walked out onto the dark sidewalk, tipped his hat and said, "My dear. We are like horseshit. We've been all over the road." Then he turned and disappeared into the night.

We did admit him to hospice. He lived with a disinterested and gruff brother-in-law who had no intention of helping take care of him. We got calls about our patient falling and he would lay on the floor for hours until his roommate decided to call us. The patient told us about imaginary children who sat at the foot of his bed, and of a big black dog that woke him up every morning at 4AM to go to the bathroom. He knew it was visions, and not real, but he was comforted by his imagination.

He was lonely. Alone by choice because he did not want his children to see his suffering. He declined to the point that he needed to move into a nursing home. He had no resources, which didn't fit his persona. So, we admitted him as a non-funded patient.

I went to see him a few days before he died. I walked into an old, worn-out nursing facility that was dark and smelled of urine. I thought, "Surely, his room is decorated with his nice things." But I walked into an empty room with fading light and dirty, pale yellow walls. There was nothing in the room, so it had the feel of a storage closet. In the corner, by the window, he lay unconscious with no more than a cheap blanket to cover him. He labored to breathe. I couldn't say anything. I stood there and cried and said goodbye in my mind. His rich stories and legendary life shattered before me. At a time when his last days should have been surrounded with bright light, laughter, and imaginary children and dogs, he was reduced to loneliness and poverty. It was his end.

Cancer comes for all walks of life, but it is still classist. Few in my days working for a hospice enjoyed the luxury of a soft focused, well-funded ending.

The following story is based on a true experience. While working with patients, I chose to only share their lives as short stories.

Everybody Dies

Shaggy stained carpets, rambling rooms of an old, worn-down house full of children of every color and age. Shadowy adults lurking on sagging couches; especially that dark, angry young man in the corner. He hurts people. He only knows one way to move through the world. The children learn. It's loud. It smells like smoke and old grease. She is frazzled and agitated as she tries to wrangle the wild and aimless children. They shout and wrestle. There's a sixteen-year-old girl holding her pregnant stomach. She looks at the children with a mixture of contempt and fear – her own child only to become one of them.

Doris knew this scene very well.

"Everybody dies," she reminded herself.

With her best cheery demeanor, she pulled up through her spine to be tall and confident. That dark man in the corner was watching with calculating eyes.

"Come on in, and let's get this over with," the frazzled woman said.

Doris sat down at an oversized picnic table that was doubling as the family dining table. The woman sat opposite of her and watched with impatience as Doris fumbled through her papers. The woman had dark circles under her eyes. What could have been mistaken as wrinkles were just the lines of exhaustion on her face. How old was she? Doris couldn't exactly tell. Doris became aware of a slight, warm presence nuzzling against her right side. She looked down to see a bedraggled little girl with shiny red hair leaning against her. The child smiled and leaned in as close as she could. Doris smiled. Her heart was breaking. She thought, "Is this the only love you'll get today?" Little boys screamed and chased each other around the house. It was a loud cacophony. It was hard to concentrate and the woman across from her was becoming more agitated. Finally, Doris laid out her forms, smoothed them with her palms and leaned in to look directly into the woman's eyes.

"So, this is your father who is dying?" she asked.

"Yeah." The response was so matter of fact.

"Do you understand what's going on? What hospice is?"

"Yeah, I'm a nurse."

This surprised Doris. Certainly, she had met less than professional "nurses" in various facilities throughout the area, but this woman seemed as unlikely as any. "I see. Then what we'll need to do is go over some basic information and then I'll have you sign the proper paperwork to get services started."

A fight was breaking out in the living room between two of the boys. One was much bigger than the other. They shouted and shoved. There was a dull, seemingly deadly thunk. Doris looked up to see the smaller boy's head slammed against a door frame. For an instant he went limp. The woman across from her registered rage, instinctively raised her fist, then caught herself, feigned a look of concern and asked, "Dillon, you O.K.?"

"Yes, Mama."

"No crying. We don't cry around here, right," she asked with an undertone of menace.

"No. Mama."

With that, she looked back at Doris, apologized for the commotion and asked her to continue. Doris did her best to be as unaffected as the woman. She explained hospice services, asked the woman if she had any questions so far, and the woman quickly said, "Nope. Where do I sign?" Doris got it. This needed to hurry up, so she pulled out an Informed Consent form and asked the woman to look over it, initial in the proper places and sign. As the woman quickly glanced and signed, Doris explained bereavement services.

"They'll be available to anyone in your family."

The woman registered some glint of interest. Then asked if there was anything else she needed to sign.

Doris continued the process of signing up a man she had yet to see to hospice care. She finally asked, "Is your father here in this home?"

Without looking up from the papers, the woman said, "Yeah. He's back there. He's sleeping and he don't like to be bothered."

"O.K.," Doris replied. "The nurse will be here in a while to finish the admission. She will have to spend some time with him."

"That's fine," the woman agreed as she pushed the rest of the papers back at Doris.

Doris got up to leave, expecting to have to let herself out, but to her surprise, the woman said, "I'll walk you out. It's late and this ain't a friendly neighborhood."

As they walked towards the door, Doris glanced at the group of adults sitting around the living room. The pregnant girl stared straight ahead with her lips taught with the slightest suggestion of fear. The young man watched Doris with suspicion. She was happy to get out of that house.

Once on the porch, the woman seemed to relax. She pulled a pack of cigarettes out of her robe, lit one, inhaled deeply and sighed out the smoke. Then she smiled.
"You know. I journal. That's what they say to do. It helps me do the right thing."

"The right thing?" Doris asked.

"Take care of Daddy."

"Well, he's lucky to have you." It seemed like such a stupid thing to say to this very worn-down woman.

"He killed my mama."

Without even thinking, Doris said, "You're a hell of a lot stronger than me." Then she immediately corrected herself, "I'm sorry. I shouldn't have said that."

The woman smiled. "Nah. It's O.K. It's just the way it is. This family..." She trailed off as she lifted the cigarette to her lips. It was quiet for a few minutes. Then she continued. "He was doing life. But since he ain't gonna live much longer with that cancer and all, they said he could come on home if I'd watch after him." She looked right at Doris and seemed to be pleading more than asking, "Things just happen, you know?"

Doris didn't know, but she answered, "I guess."

The woman motioned back into the house with her cigarette. She exhaled a puff of smoke and shook her head. "That boy in there. Sittin' in the corner. He adores my daddy. It's the only positive role model he ever had. I know he'll run when Daddy dies. Won't be able to find him. Jail probably."

Doris reeled at that. A positive role model? It was beyond her comprehension. She was struggling to find a response. Her mind was racing for logic. Nothing but violence. No man to be counted on; except to harm them. Love that runs deep with dysfunction. The cycle in motion. The front door opened, and the pregnant girl stepped onto the porch. She walked directly to Doris and stood as close as she could without touching. She wrapped her arms around herself in a protective way.

"Are you looking for comfort? Do you need to run away? Escape? Will you be different if you do?" These questions rolled around in Doris' head like an avalanche. This was about to get deep. Deeper than she knew how to go, so she resumed her cheery position from earlier and said, "Well! You can expect that nurse to come around soon. Have a lovely evening." She started down the steps with the girl following her. The girl waited as Doris got into the car. Doris knew she wanted her to roll down the window. Her eyes pleaded. She continued to shelter herself in her own arms.

"Mama! He's callin' you! Get in here." It was the young man, leaning against an open front door. The girl looked towards him, looked back at Doris, her fear deepened, then she quickly walked back into the house with the woman.

Doris sat in the drive for a few minutes longer, fighting back tears. She closed her eyes, started the car, and reminded herself, "Everybody dies."

The poor die in the shadows. Left with rejection from renowned cancer clinics that seem to have no use for "garden variety" cancers that hold no promise of a new discovery for their cure. These people go home with apologies and not much more. When the hospital lets the hospice know the person is on the way home, they don't give up much more than an address and history and physical.

I've seen drug dealers pool at the end of a street where an impoverished woman is dying. Her pain can only be controlled with morphine. That morphine will be jerked from her within minutes of any hospice personnel's departure. Then we struggle to keep her comfortable. We'll pray the electric company holds off on cutting power until she dies. We file her quiet resolve in the corner of our minds where emotional pain and trauma reside.

To a corporate hospice, that finely dressed, lonely gentleman or that dying impoverished woman were numbers. A census metric. A person who will get no more than necessary to meet federal guidelines of care. No narrative about their needs for more. For safety and compassion to get through. They are no more than a high five in a Monday morning standup.

Sure. A wealthy businessman is slated for the same bare minimum treatment, but his status and his income will mitigate that from happening. The likelihood of more visits, better medications and a willing volunteer to visit are way better. And if the hospice can't provide it, he will get it elsewhere. He isn't as reliant on hospice as hospice is reliant on him and his family's probable memorial donation to the hospice's foundation after his passing.

I wanted every patient to have comfort and peace, but I would work 14-hour days for the poor ones. I did what I could to bridge the gap of ambivalence towards their lives. So, when the local chapter of Relay for Life approached me for a corporate sponsorship for their all night walking event, I didn't hesitate to say yes. I knew it would be all walks of life on that track. Class would dissolve into the wee hours of the night as families and community members took turns walking the walk of hope, sadness and defiance.

The next morning, I approached the manager of our local hospice branch with the proposal to offer up a $2000 corporate sponsorship of the event. I got a fast, "no," and no matter how I argued for it, the answer didn't change. At this time, I was too unaware of corporate spending to understand that a tiny Texas town's population wasn't worth a corporate sponsorship. Too few people would see the advertising. But honestly, it was a drop in the bucket for a nationwide company. I also understood that it opened the floodgates for other local organizations to ask for support. Corporations that operate in small towns don't understand that, and there's no appetite for a solution to address it. I wasn't winning the argument for a $2000 sponsorship and finally the manager said, "Why do you try so hard for these people anyway?"

And right there, my life became something very different. My life goals crystallized, and my style of leadership was born. I got up and walked out of her office. I had a porch. I had a long list of musicians that had become friends, and I knew which ones would back me up if I created an event that raised that money but also poked the corporation in the eye.

Premise: Extreme suffering creates a champion

Leadership Lesson: The greatest organizations and movements are sparked by the disruption of compassion and care for humanity. If a company cannot create genuine pride and motivation in your heart, it's not really a disruption. Founders with a passion for their mission and humanity are the true disrupters because they aren't afraid to say, "This needs to change."

Chapter 6
The Peace from the Porch Project

These lyrics wove in and out of each other in polyphony when the Bear Creek Ensemble was formed.

Hallelujah for this day
A passing smile, a friendly glance, a wave hello
I will breathe in anger, and I will breathe out love

Those lyrics would skate across the top of a chorus in a way that tangled them into a complex melody that would become the earworm of 2004.

Chorus:
I will not surrender
I will not back down
I will not be pulled under and I won't be pushed around
I resolve to live this day the very best I can
'Cause I know I'll never get a chance to live this day again

Stacy Lieder wrote those lyrics. She was the sound engineer for Bear Creek Concerts. She was an extraordinary songwriter and had been my partner in the amazing community scene we built all those many Tuesday nights ago in College Station. Now we were on a mission of good unlike any we had ever participated in. We would create the original Bear Creek Ensemble to record songs for a benefit album called "Peace from the Porch, Vol. 1"

"Peace from the Porch" was my benediction at the end of every Bear Creek Concert. It's how I ended emails and newsletters. Sometimes I stretched it into something like, "From the middle of a hayfield, in the middle of Fayette County, in the middle of Texas, in the middle of America, Peace from the Porch."

Little actions and small events can blossom, and the Peace from the Porch Project did.

One of the hospice nurses that I worked with was as appalled by our manager's comment as me, and she was a deeply giving woman driven by her profound Christian faith. She and her husband ponied up $1000. I would raise the rest and more. Dana and Charlie also happened to be amazing singers in their church's praise band. Naturally, they would be part of the Bear Creek Ensemble. Dana and Stacy can find harmonies in thin air. Both have perfected the craft of harmonizing, but to do it the way they can is to be born with a gift for it. This was exciting. We would record in layered harmonies and polyphones.

I had such a passion in me that I didn't want our recordings to be anything less than the very best Austin had to offer, so we headed to Congress House with Mark Hallman and recorded two songs. In the meantime, I had solicited 7 songwriters to contribute a song or two to the CD. The compilation would have a signature Bear Creek Concert sound, featuring some of the crowd favorites.

Most artists to "play the porch" were songwriters who performed acoustic sets. Until I started working on Peace from the Porch, Vol.1, there had never been more than 3 performers on the porch at a time. Most artists came alone and gave personal performances with voice and guitar. The genres were Folk, Americana and Blues. It was rootsy music in a wide-open rural setting.

Once we had established a core audience, I had a good idea of which artists were their favorites, and those are the ones I invited to join the project. They didn't have to record anything new. I asked for previously recorded songs that I could use for a compilation. Only the newly formed Bear Creek Ensemble would present newly recorded music. We recorded Stacy's tune, "Affirmation," that I cited at the beginning of the chapter and an old song of mine that had never been recorded called, "There is a Place." Wendy had given the song its title because the lyrics were about universal connection somewhere beyond our planet. Both songs lend themselves to rich harmonies, so we kept the musical accompaniment simple and let the voices create the emotional punch.

Once Mark had the ensemble mixed, I sent him the rest of the song contributions and let him master it in a smooth warm way that felt like the living room of the cabin. We had created an album that would appeal to small town locals as well as the greater folk and acoustic music world.

There is so much more than anyone could ever imagine that goes into creating a CD. From my tiny office in the cabin guest quarter, I set to doing almost all the legwork myself. I wouldn't make any money from this project, and in fact, it would end up costing me about $2000. For someone making a meager salary, this seemed crazy, but something in my gut told me to "give into the god."

Here's a lesson in leadership - Give into the God

What does that mean? Firstly, I say "the god" because there are many beliefs or non-beliefs about a god. For me, it is a source I don't even try to wrap my head around, but I do know we have some unspoken and hard to understand calling to put positivity into the universe. To tithe into the mystery. For me, it was The Peace from the Porch Project. Some said my karma bank was very full; others were confused as to why I would work so hard for no financial gain. A leader gives into the god. They give more than they take from their purpose. They don't think about monetary success, but rather think about building legacies and empowering people to lift humanity in some kind of movement or work. If you're in a job that is strictly about the money, it can really put a dirty film on your conscience.

Giving into the god is really just another component of servant leadership. Most people won't put the level of work I did into something like Peace from the Porch, Vol 1, but many people can be inspired to get involved and do their part. Servant leaders inspire because it's this source or god that drives them. No matter how much criticism or complaining I heard about spending money I didn't really have, I never let up. I was determined to make that CD and raise money for Relay for Life. I had something to prove, and dammit, I was going to do it with every ounce of passion I could squeeze out of the hospice patient experiences I had been a part of. This kind of leader is not afraid to work their tail off. What this leader doesn't know, they will learn if it's necessary to achieve a goal. Their personal presentation can get sloppy from the hard work. It's the desire and focus within their spirit that makes them shine. I probably spent most of the Peace from the Porch Project in cutoffs and hiking boots. Creating a musical movement is dirty work with long hours.

I discovered that I could pull energy out of the depths of my psyche and work a forty hour week for hospice and still put in an extra four to six hours a night to finish the CD. I needed a creative voice to write the liner notes, and I needed to be organized to keep artist agreements up-to-date and valid. I had to sequence the CD.

Sequencing is choosing the order of the songs. I learned from Mark that a well sequenced album pulls the listener along like a good story. It starts in a low key and moves up the scale. It has to have just the right amount of energy and punch in the beginning to engage the listener. I had to be careful about slow songs. Too many at once loses the audience. And there had to be some arc to the whole thing that settled into a satisfying ending. Even the unseen work that goes into creating an album has a premise. "Common purpose and passion leads to victory."

It paid off. We beat our fundraising goal. We sold out of CDs. We hosted two stages at the Houston International Festival, and we closed the Bear Creek Concert season with a multi-artist event to promote Peace from the Porch, Vol. 1. We won a MTM Texas Music Award for Musical Event of the Year, and that award was the first of several that honored music and community fundraising. We led a revolution to make a difference with a community of regional musicians that could take all their musical hard work and turn it into something valuable beyond the clubs and music stores.

Now I had a foothold and a responsibility to uphold what I had begun. There would be Vol. 2 and Vol. 3. Vol 2 would send us back to the International Festival where we would pack the area around our stage with music fans who would, in turn, buy that CD and help us fund the Houston Women's Center.

Peace from the Porch Vol. 1 had been so successful that I was able to secure funding from corporate Texas grocery giant, H-E-B, to sponsor the Vol. 2 stage at the International Festival. With that financial support, I could cover travel and lodging for performers across the country. Of course, H-E-B had a few performer requests that played our stage, too.

Although most won't know who they are, real indie music fans and songwriting aficionados will understand that we were creating quite the mini festival within the International Festival Grounds. We presented:

Ruthie Foster
Patrice Pike

Erika Luckett (1965 - 2018)
Shake Russell
Eric Taylor (1949 - 2020)

All were well known and respected singer/songwriters that drew crowds to our stage and helped us sell CDs.

Along with their ability to create a festival draw, we also included every other artist that donated songs to Vol. 2. It was a two-weekend event that once again required our dedicated team of volunteers to pull off. We not only had sound to set up and run, but we had a portable green room for the musicians and a merchandise booth. Our days started at 7AM and ran until two hours after the festival gates closed. Instead of one act, I had multiple acts to manage each day. It was a test of my ability to coordinate their load ins, performance and load outs, all while the next set of performers were queuing up. With musicians, part of managing a multi-artist event is just tracking them down, as not all are good with punctuality. It's an exercise in being everywhere at once.

Because I had the H-E-B sponsorship, I was able to move the top drawing performers over to the Kerrville Folk Festival stage to help improve their presence. They didn't have the budget to pay much, so I could inflate pay enough to cover both stages. In turn (and this is really important on a hot Houston weekend), we had access to their flushing toilets.

I had complete faith in my volunteer team to manage everything else. I gave them complete autonomy to manage their own duties, and together, we pulled off a perfect event. It was so successful that we were able to send a very nice check to the Houston Women's Center. It was where the whole Peace from the Porch volunteer team earned the "living legend" status; not just me.

Somewhere between Vol. 1 and Vol. 2, I resigned from that corporate hospice company and moved to a rural non-profit hospice. My reputation was strong, and I was able to fundraise big checks and even a donated building that became one of the offices for Hospice Brazos Valley. How did I do it? I was fueled by the patients and their stories. I let my involvement in community organizations drive me. But what I didn't do is bend to small town norms. In a way, it made me a threat, or shall I say, someone to fear because I was outside of their milieu.

I was the person to call for many non-hospice related crises in the community. I invested in getting to know community leaders - from the bank boards to the rundown neighborhoods and compounds of the poor. People asked for Christy, not Hospice Brazos Valley.

I had office guests who just wanted to talk about their situation or something that concerned them. I had requests to help the poor and elderly with simple "handyman" tasks. I threw an annual party for the hospice team and their families, and I let them define the term family. In some cultures, that means anyone living on the block, whether they're blood related or not. It means a second cousin. Not just immediate family. We grew into a new definition of community for a small town that didn't have much visibility beyond its white citizens.

I was easy to find, and I found myself in an unlikely partnership with an extremely poor black woman who was very active in her community. She would say, "If I got two nickels to rub together, I'm gonna share one of them."

Her name was Eva Cain. She was extremely large, loud and nosy. But her heart was pure gold, and she pulled me into her world whenever she needed extra support helping someone in an even worse situation than hers. I got a call from her one afternoon.

She said, "Come pick me up, and don't bring that damn tiny convertible of yours. Bring your truck so I can fit in it. I got something to show you."

I picked her up in my truck and she cussed about having to wear her seatbelt. She was large, and barely buckled in, but that was my one element of control with Eva. She said, "Start driving toward Whataburger, and I'll tell you where to go."

She guided me down country roads that turned into dirt lanes. As we drove, she pointed out the property for the Chicken Ranch (Best Little Whorehouse in Texas). She told me her mother managed the place for the Madame. "My mama is bigger than me, and she walked up and down the halls with a bat in one hand and an ax in the other. She'd peek in the little sliding windows in the doors of the rooms, and if someone was being rough with a girl, they better run like hell before she caught 'em."

We finally stopped at a compound of dilapidated mobile homes. They were scattered across a patch of dirt surrounded by brush, trash piles and broken down cars. "Ok," she said. "We're here to talk to this man. His wife is coming home from MD Anderson today. She has stomach cancer and they ain't doin' nothin' for her. She's coming home to die, but she can't die in there." She pointed to a trailer that looked creased, bent and rusted out. "Go on up there. That deck ain't gonna hold me."

I got out of the car and Eva called to a man inside. "She's here to help y'all!" The commotion pulled other people from their shacks. I could not believe people lived in these structures. What's worse is that I recognized many of them from stores or businesses in town. How much were they paid to do their jobs if they had to live in such unacceptable poverty? It was eye opening and devastating.

I stepped onto the deck of the man's trailer, shook his hand and introduced myself. He was gentle, shy and embarrassed. He almost whispered. He needed hot water for his wife. I walked inside and thought I was going to fall through the floor. It flexed and sagged under my feet. The kitchen area was in front of me. There appeared to have been a fire at the stove as black soot covered the walls and the broken vent hood. The sink was dirty. The counters were cluttered. The connected living room was full of boxes and there was a twin bed against the wall. The carpet was worn through to the subfloor. I could see daylight between the floor and the baseboards as the old trailer was beginning to separate from itself. I asked to see the bedroom and bathroom.

"We sleep right here." He pointed to the twin bed. I was taking mental notes of what they would need to survive, but not much more than that. I was also working hard to keep my expression calm and friendly. I replied, "Ok. We'll get you a double mattress."

He showed me the dirty little bathroom that looked unusable. There was a small room at the end of a narrow hall. The place was sweltering. I asked if he had A/C and he said no. I asked if he had electricity. He did. Then I asked to see the hot water heater. He said it was outside. So, before I went out to check it, I opened the cabinets under the kitchen sink to see if the pipes were intact. I stuck my head and upper body in the space and was swarmed with cockroaches.

Let me stop here and let you know that my irrational fear is roaches. I had heard stories from hospice nurses about homes so infested with roaches that the bugs would crawl across the patient. I have no idea how I kept my calm demeanor as I backed out of the cabinets, but I did. I knew I'd probably do a jig when I got home as I stripped in my front yard. I went outside to check the water heater. It was rusted out and useless. I made my list. A window unit for the common area, a double mattress, a new hot water heater, food, sheets, and a reinforced floor. It was still an inhospitable dump, but I could make it better without pulling them from their community. I knew that their definition of family was that broken down compound, and I should meet them where they were at.

I found Eva socializing in a common yard area, and we headed back to town. I dropped her off at her home and raced to my house, wiping at my neck and arms and checking the interior of my truck for bugs.

The next day, I delivered my list of needs and my story to the local Rotary Club. They took care of everything, including rebuilding the trailer floor. We didn't give that family much, but that very sick woman was able to come home and die clean and with some dignity.

My work was bittersweet. I felt proud of myself that I was a trusted resource, but I hated that so many members of the community went home to unspeakable poverty. The kind that produces minimum wage and keeps one alive, but also keeps that person from truly living.

I had to leave that rural job because it wasn't exactly appreciated by the home office that people called the hospice office in La Grange, Texas "Christy's hospice." No one ever asked, "how do you do it? How do you get such solid support?" Instead, I was seen as diluting the brand. That's a lesson for me that I can share with you.

If you're becoming too visible, you must find a way to lay low or you have to move on. Although I had perfected the behind-the-scenes job of musical production, I was too visible and vocal for healthcare. I moved on. My legacy was a strong hospice presence in a community far from most resources, and an appreciation by the people who worked with me. I hope I showed that little town a different way to make a difference because it was time for me to return to Austin.

No one ever taught me how to be a leader. I didn't take leadership courses or management classes. I am self-taught, and therefore, more rogue than most companies can handle. I am disruptive, but not in the cool techy sense of the word. I disrupt the disruptors because those tech disruptors aren't all that good at leading people. At the same time, they hold their ideas and companies close and tend to micromanage because they believe they're protecting their brilliance. I think that's very much human nature.

Startup companies like Austin because it's a town full of recent college graduates and transplants who came for the music and hiking. It's a low wage pool of workers who agree to a low salary to hold onto the Austin quality of life. I spent my first year back in the city freelance writing, editing, maintaining websites and consulting. I loved the freedom, but the income was terrible. It was the time of content farms that paid the lowest wage because they really didn't care if the writing was good if it hit the optimal number of keywords to flood the search engines. Most website owners that hired me had very little money, so they paid poorly while asking for way more than that money could buy.

It was a weird time. Peace from the Porch Vol. 3 had launched, but without the Bear Creek Cabin, it just didn't have the punch of Vol. 1 and Vol. 2. There's an arc to everything, and I was sliding to the bottom of mine. It was time to go back to corporate work, and I hated that.

Another tip: Success ebbs and flows. Celebrate the wins, but don't let bench time derail you. It should be a time of reflection. A time to observe the successes of others and learn. I tell you this because I failed at this advice. I didn't even notice myself drifting away from my style of servant leadership, and my mission to give into the god. A job with a small tech company was going to begin the process of completely altering my brain.

My biggest mistake was letting go of my community. Leaders do not operate in a vacuum. They don't sit on a throne, looking down on minions. They are surrounded by equals and examples and mentors. I was choking on a weird kind of grief for what had been, and it was dimming the light on my "now." I was able to let go of the physical porch. I had yet to understand that it was figurative, and therefore standing strong. That would take a lot of years to sink in for me.

A Brief Interlude

When I think about my idea of a great leader, a few things come to mind.

Compassion with a direct line of availability - People need people, and sometimes they need a person who can guide them through a hard patch in life. I'm not saying the boss or all leaders should drop the mission for a group hug, but the willingness to do it if it comes to that is an attribute very few people, who fancy themselves to be a leader, possess. When I think about compassion as a leadership trait, I think of it as the hardest trait to master. How do you ride the line between caring and keeping enough distance to continue to lead? Start by listening. Then be connected to the right resources to outsource the support if you need to. That may be an HR partner or a healthcare option or in some cases, you.

Speak up - This is for everyone. Not just people in management or traditional leadership roles. The rank and file in a company tend to mumble among themselves when they see the company making a bad decision; especially when the work they do is affected by the decision. In large companies (and probably many small ones), leadership isn't familiar with the intricacies of operations. They rely on the team to know, understand and execute for them. However, when it comes to bad decisions that are often spawned due to that lack of deep knowledge, the team keeps quiet. If you have a strong enough opinion to blast a company chat channel, then share that opinion with leadership. Be prepared to defend your opinion, and when you get dismissed, because you will, take that as the challenge not only to speak up but stand up and prove yourself. Maybe ask a question like, "Is the company making this decision from a purely financial point of view, or is there something going on with company strategy that I should know about in order to help you meet that goal?" But be prepared to give solid evidence of why you have a concern. And gather your workmates to present a solution. I think we tend to wait for permission to shine. I know I'm guilty of that. For whatever reason, I was reluctant to present a different way to do things. I fell prey to the idea that rocking the boat would cost me my job. It eventually did, and now hindsight is 20/20. I should have spoken up and stood up to many leadership teams prior to the one that decided it was time to cull the old guard.

Be honest with yourself - I'm going to be honest with the reader first. Realizing that the job you have is not the right job for you is terrifying. It's incredibly hard to find a new job that will fill your professional bucket. Striking out on your own is even harder. We're not all built for that. Even so, it's incredibly important to be honest with yourself. If for no other reason, honesty can help you recalibrate and sustain the job you currently have. I just caution you to know that you can't make recalibration a routine thing. I made that mistake, and it wore me out mentally. Recalibrate and start building your exit plan. If you're in a leadership role, make sure that any recalibration includes your team. They rely on you, so don't abandon them.

Don't chicken out - If your recalibration opens a window of opportunity, don't let it close on you. Try. Commit. Believe in yourself. This sounds so trope-like. I guarantee you that I could put "Try. Commit. Believe in yourself" on a plaque in a roadside convenience store, and people would buy it. It's like Tony Robbins tucked between the cigarettes and lotto tickets. Easy to say, but really hard to do. Mostly because it's hard work, and of course, you're probably worn out from your day job. Even if you can only sustain it for thirty minutes a day, do it. Make a commitment to yourself to explore something better. It could be learning a new skill. It could be writing. It could be building a business plan for your own idea. It could be showing your current leadership team a new way of thinking and executing on company goals. Just don't give up on it. Those windows don't open every day.

Give change a chance - I think most unhappy workers exist in a state of desperation that simply doesn't lend itself to moving on to something new and better. So, here's what to do: Give change a chance. Don't react negatively as soon as you see change happening around you. Yep. It often feels negative and defeating but lay low and just let that change happen. It could be that you simply don't do well with change, and you're not alone if your job is in the trenches where that change creates the most work. And that brings me to my final thought.

What is the material impact of your daily tasks? - This is the spring cleaning of operational work. Change, new ideas, misguided initiatives bring new tasks to teams. Teams don't get bigger just because the workload is growing. A good leader assesses the department's work and stops any task that doesn't produce meaningful outcomes. If the work is another department's "honey do list," you can probably stop doing it. If no one ever asks about it or indicates a task is still needed, stop doing it. If the task produces no revenue or even a correlation to revenue, ditch it. Make room for work that produces positive key results. Burning a team out with too many tasks isn't a positive key result.

Premise: Common causes choose teams. Hiring Managers choose employees.

Leadership Lesson: Don't wait to be asked to lead. Simply do it. There are no instructions, and the best leaders won't need them anyway.

Chapter 7
The Trees Are Tired

I meditated daily while living at Bear Creek. I could sit for 45 minutes and transcend into a state of absolute peace. Once I returned to the city, it was my intention to continue my meditation practice, but I found I simply couldn't do it. I was easily distracted and agitated. Even quiet walks around the lake didn't calm me. I told a friend about this, and I concluded, "the trees are tired" in the city.

Trees are silent observers as much as they are providers. I told myself that too much toxicity and funky energy had worn them out. There was no easy flow, only turbulence.

Time for a story.

The Staircase Hauntings

I don't want to believe in ghosts, but this thing has been following me around for a lifetime.

It started when I was five. There was something about the hollow space underneath my grandmother's staircase that made me leap over the third and fourth steps. My people are practical people. They do not believe in ghosts or allow their children to believe in ghosts. So, I never told anyone about my daily leap. My terror grew as I realized the haunting had moved into the deep, dark closet in my room at my grandmother's house. Now it could wait for me to fall asleep, but it knew I'd lie there paralyzed with fear. I couldn't close my eyes because it would get me. I couldn't bolt down the stairs because it was faster than me, and it would just position itself under step number three to grab my wobbly ankle as I raced down the steps, through the living room door, and into the warmth of the kitchen. It was a well-planned haunting. So don't think ghosts don't think. They do. And this one followed me to college.

Texas A&M University is like my family. Practical. No room for the paranormal or mystical; unless, of course, you believe a bonfire will control the outcome of a football game. But it's a big, powerful school. They have ways around their own superstitions. For me, the problem was much more personal and real. Stupidly, I picked a house to rent that had a staircase. That ghost followed me there and set up residence as if my new set of stairs was a comfortable old shoe. The hauntings commenced immediately. I had a paranoid, drug addict for a roommate, and the ghost knew he would be easy prey. Johnnie couldn't tell a bad acid trip from paranormal bullying. Instead of lurking under the stairs, the entity tended to loiter in the stairwell itself. This old cottage had one of those tightly enclosed staircases that's about four feet wide with dark paneled walls. It was about as creepy as they come. At the age of twenty, I could still clear thirteen steps in two leaps. The old fear from Grandmother's house was in good shape when it came to an aerobic ascent to the upstairs bathroom. Johnnie simply refused to come downstairs for days at a time. The ghost also took up with living creatures. It preferred the company of roaches and rats. They moved in and lingered in the stairwell, too. I could hear them scuttling in the walls. Sometimes one would zip through the kitchen, and they held convention in throbbing masses on the trunk of the old oak tree out front. A more grounded individual would have told me that I was not suffering from a haunting, but from a hefty case of student poverty. No matter. I knew the truth, the ghost was my life mate, and it would always be there to give me a healthy dose of chronic fear and uncertainty.

As Texas A&M faded into the back room of my young adulthood, and an actual career pulled me out of student poverty, I bought a nice piece of property in the country. I built a house on a hayfield that was backed by twenty acres of woods. Why I thought that ghost wouldn't find my woods to be the perfect playground, I don't know. It moved right in, preferring to lurk just on the edge of the trees near the well house. It liked to blow up its energetic meanness and spook me into a sprint for the house whenever I was forced to go to that little well house for any night time business. Naturally, it was faster than me, and it mastered the ability to haunt the very walls of my home. It took up a new practice. In the wee hours of the morning, I would be awakened by the distant sound of AM radio. This ghost was a fan of 1950's rock n' roll. Since I'm an independent music producer and writer, I came to understand that the ghost chose me for a reason. It was time to make my peace with the paranormal and let it be my friend.

All I had to do was think, "Be my friend," at 3 a.m. on a balmy spring night, and the fear lifted. That doesn't mean my ghost no longer haunts, but now I'm in on the joke. We know that the best way to get rid of an unwanted house guest is to send them up the stairs in my country home. By step three they'll sense the fear. By step four, they'll be certain there's an evil claw wrapped around an ankle. By step five, they will have decided they don't like me, and they will leave forever.

This ghost could get me through the kind of divorce where I get it all. All it has to do is grab an ankle. I love my ghost. Tonight, we'll hum a few bars of "Love Me Tender" before I drift off to sleep.

We create illusions within ourselves to cope with loss, rejection, negative self-talk, and imposter syndrome.

I blamed it on the trees. Today I can accept that there are arcs in life that follow the natural pendulum of time. We rise. We fall. We gather the momentum to catch the next upswing. The tricky part is finding the energy to make the effort.

To walk away from Bear Creek was more emotionally devastating than I ever imagined. I had wrapped my identity into the porch. If there was a ghost still there, it was me. A part of me still lives there, and I guarantee that the walls of that cabin sing to the new owners. The wood was full of vibrations of songs. A quality guitar will improve with age. As sound vibrations buzz across its wood, there is a transformation. All of the conversations, music, and sounds of living wiggle into the grains of wood to give the instrument its unique sound. With its wood slat walls, the Bear Creek Cabin would certainly hold its history within the grain.

It is a living organism that was built for music and good works. I know nothing about the family that bought it, but I hope they were possessed by the spirit of the porch. That energy was at home there. It didn't follow me back to Austin. I was an emotional vacuum as I struggled to readapt to city living.

Country towns v. cities. The energies are very different. The lifestyles, the jobs, the creativity, the people. Upon my return to Austin, I convinced myself that I had been a big fish in a little pond, and I was currently at the low point in the swing. I had let go of the wrong things. I was keenly aware of my own mental energy. My constant creativity. I wrote songs in that first year back in the city. I wrote for a living. And I gave up my drive to lead for a noble purpose. Life became survival. No room for growth according to my self-talk.

The trees were probably fine. It was me that was tired. I could feel myself start to spiral. I directed my attention to a social life that wasn't honest. I spent too much time reliving college days with old friends from A&M. Nights were full of restaurants, beer and revelry. It was not what I needed to fill the void in me, but it was how I coped. I left no time for reason in my mind. I wouldn't allow myself to simply stop and meditate. The trees were tired.

Finally, I had to "get a real job" to support myself. Freelancing was good for healing, and had I continued, I may have worked out my weird brand of grief and recalibrated my commitment to The Peace from the Porch project and what it represented. But freelancing isn't really much more profitable than playing music for a living. Regardless of any need to create, my overblown sense of personal responsibility kicked in and sent me on the path towards better income.

Austin was a start-up town in 2012. One of my writing clients was still billing itself as a start-up. They needed operational staff, so I applied and got a job in an industry I knew absolutely nothing about. Tech, ecommerce, marketing.

When I interviewed for the job, I went through 6 different interviews in one day. Looking back on it, that was ridiculous. I was taking an entry level job. My place was among recent graduates. Why on earth was I interviewing with everyone from a potential peer to the CEO? I was in my mid-40s, and I thought, "My god. What are they doing beyond this room that's so top secret and important that 6 people with ascending titles have to interview me?" By the 6th hour, and final interview with the CEO, I can honestly say that I did not give a shit.

He was gruff. He was arrogant. He was clearly self-important. He had no people skills. I did my best to see him and communicate with him as a peer because it was clear he thought he was intimidating me. He wasn't. He's the kind of guy you decide to work for only because you're in desperate need of a steady paycheck, and I was. During the interview he admitted that Austin was a great startup town because there was an endless supply of cheap labor coming out of the University of Texas. Clearly, the pay was going to be crap.

They offered me the job with an embarrassingly low salary. Actually, they bumped me up by $4,000 because I was older and more experienced. They wanted to know why I wasn't applying for a management position, and that surprised me because I honestly had no real idea of what kind of job I was applying for. Today, looking back on it, I should have said I'd take a management job. Sure. I can do that.

Here's a leadership lesson. Learn the job before you commit to leading. If I had taken a management job without a clue to what I would be responsible for, I would have met employee resistance on day one. There would have been zero respect for me or what I could offer because a group of young recent grads don't think that way. Many companies don't care. This particular company had a hefty turnover rate, and I don't think me coming in as the new "boss" was going to slow the churn. I came in as a peer, learned enough about what the team did, and how the team operated (as a team, which it wasn't doing), and then made my proposal.

I was on the production team. What that means is that I was on a team of six people who processed coupon codes from affiliate marketing feeds that served as the middleman between online retailers and coupon publishing sites. It was an eye-crossingly boring job. I was really good at it. Once I understood the editorial style guide of how to edit the data, I could handle a very large volume of work without stressing much at all. If it paid better, I probably would have been perfectly happy to do that simple job for years, but it paid badly and there increasingly became more tasks asked of the team that weren't so simple. It was clear that this group of workers was smart and way more capable than the company realized, but they were young and unsupported.

The team's director was a drunk. He was gone within a week of me being hired. The team lead never helped me at all. A peer trained me. He was gone after some disagreement with the CEO. He must have resigned but left immediately. That was a pretty clear signal that top leadership was not very good. If it had been, the middle managers and team leads would have been much better. At the director level, it was clear the company wasn't good at vetting for a self-destructive personality. At the team lead level, there was too much micromanaging around tasks that the leadership team only understood from the periphery. It was as if smart people with potential were a threat rather than an asset.

Even so, I made my proposal to the VP over the production team. I said, "I know I told you I wasn't interested in management when you interviewed me, but I think you need me." He did, and after a brief stint as a co-team lead. I was promoted to department manager.

There was this innocent belief on the team that everyone had to stay at their desk until 6PM every day. Even if there was no work to do, they needed to stay. On day one, after the announcement that I was their new manager, I spun my chair around to face them and said, "This 6PM on Friday rule is bullshit. When you're done, go enjoy your weekend. Even if it's only 4PM." I have never believed in clock punching. I learned that from that boss way back in my eye care management days. "If you can get your job done in 4 hours, and you can produce outstanding results, it's ok to leave. Go do something you enjoy."

Productivity improved. Trust was established. We could now start our journey towards excellence and operational expertise.

Premise: Core principles do not change for good leaders.

Leadership Lesson: Let the things you don't understand be your launch pad. If you think like a leader, you can handle anything.

Chapter 8
<u>Work Ethic was a Career Killer</u>

How do you turn around a demoralized team in an industry you know very little about?

Pay attention.

People will tell you what you need to know if you really pay attention.

I was responsible for 5 people who had been regularly ignored, devalued and even blamed for mistakes they didn't make. So, one of a few things were going on. One spent her day gossiping and scrolling through social media and memes. Two were taking on everything they could to show their worth (and this was foreshadowing of how the entire team would eventually operate), and one was wrapped up in toxic personal drama. I knew my challenge was to save who I could in order to hang onto the legacy knowledge the team would offer. Honestly. I am not a fan of constant hiring and training. I much prefer to keep a team intact and only let them go when a better opportunity comes along for them.

Since I hadn't been there long, I hadn't established any support from other departments or their leads. I was still learning what they did and how it related to my team. My early impression was that there was an insulated engineering team that pretty much did what they wanted. They stuck together. They stayed after work to play games on one of the conference room TVs. They never talked to me. In fact, I found it weird that no one at the company really made much effort to introduce themselves. I would encounter a stranger in the breakroom and say "hello" and introduce myself only to get a dismissive "hello" back as if that person was surprised that anyone would talk to them outside of their own department.

The age gap between me and most of the staff was also a challenge. I found myself cramming on current pop culture in order to relate to even my own team. No one knew that I was in my forties. I am lucky enough to look younger than my age. I decided there was no need to advertise it.

I think one of the things I was unfamiliar with was how much the generations below mine used text, social media and non-verbal communication. I used those things, but certainly not as a primary form of communicating. I had catching up to do to meet my team and the rest of the company where they were at. Honestly. If communication was becoming primarily chat and email, remote work should have become a viable option in 2012. However, a modern form of communication did not sync up with the old-fashioned leadership distrust of workers that I experienced in the mid-nineties. There is nothing more counterproductive than distrust. I was in an environment of rampant distrust, and therefore a constant search for someone else to blame.

In a suspicious environment, different workers will handle it in different ways. I still think more verbal and face to face communication (and I don't mean meetings), would have strengthened the staff and even my team. In non-verbal isolation, workers will manifest a common behavior to simply survive.

The two people on my team, who were working themselves to death, would need my empathy. The one who was in her own drama would need a path towards the door rather than me firing her. The one who came to work to play needed to be saved first. She was smart and she had fantastic merchandising instincts. Page merchandising was one of my team's duties. We were responsible for making sure pages on our website were optimized for the greatest return. Someone who knows what consumers get excited about was needed. Currently, this employee didn't trust me. I was new. I was an unknown, and there was no guarantee I would support anyone on the team. She never looked at me and spent much of her time typing furiously into a chat platform. One day, I turned to her and said, "I really need your help. I am terrible at merchandising, and I need someone who really understands Macy's and Nordstrom to optimize those pages."

She looked completely surprised. I continued, "You're going to be really good at that, so would you mind taking responsibility for them?"

That's all it took.

I knew she knew fashion and trends. I knew she knew customer instincts. Without her having to tell me, I showed that I knew her best attributes, and she became the best merchandiser she could be, even optimizing new page campaigns. We became friends. I earned her trust and respect. I didn't think she'd stick around long, but that was ok as long as I could just get some of her talent while she was there. I knew she'd never overwork, and that meant I would need to manage that expectation with the rest of the team. Leadership is a balancing act. It's part inspiring people to perform, and part managing the expectations of others. That takes communication.

I had come to know the team's strengths and weaknesses. I wasn't new at managing people, so I knew that team members would rather have people unfamiliar with their tasks stay away. Otherwise, it could end up creating more work for them. So, I knew the other team members wouldn't be too ruffled if this one person simply did her required volume of merchandising each day. She wasn't going to do one more page than she had to, but at least the pages she did touch would perform well. Not everyone is good at page merchandising. The two hardest workers were, in one case, a great writer, and in the other case a fantastic problem solver. It was as simple as "y'all focus on what you do well and let her merchandise."

This approach meant that the team's overall expertise grew fast, and we moved from the workers in the corner that no one cared about to the foundation of operations that no one could do without.

Of course, there's more to it than defining and empowering a team. I also had work to do with other department leads. Especially the paid marketing team. That team relied on my team to make a return on their marketing bids. If they believed my team wasn't merchandising correctly or writing good SEO copy or building proper affiliate links, they were coming for a war. So, I walked over one day and surprised those leads with this question. "I want to know what we can do to better help you. I know you rely on us to execute a successful campaign. Is there anything that would help us work together better?"

The looks on their faces were part confusion and part stunned silence. But after it passed, they were excited to work with me to create reporting that benefitted both teams, and they would bring us suggestions as well as listen to our suggestions. Over the years, that paid marketing team became my team's closest ally as the company grew and experienced the bumps and crashes that come with that.

We worked together to create complex reporting that relied on algorithms to identify where the most opportunity for growth was across thousands of pages and merchants. We developed processes that ensured nothing got overlooked and that accountability was built into the flow of collaboration. We educated each other on the work we did and what it entailed. It created respect and camaraderie. By 2015, our little company had a paid search approach that turned it into a valuable company, and we were acquired by an international corporation..

But let me back up. This chapter is about how work ethic can become a career killer. The merchandiser did leave, as I knew she would. I started hiring my own team. I didn't worry about technical backgrounds or online marketing experience. I hired people who were creative and very good at critical thinking. For the most part, I hired Liberal Arts majors. English, Art, History. There's something about that kind of mindset that just worked for the operations team. I hired one Science major, and her attention to minutiae and ability to focus on large amounts of data made her a great fit. Their personalities were all different. They came from different backgrounds, but they bonded together to work at a pace and expertise that earned me a strange compliment that was a foreshadowing of my future. "Don't worry about her and her team. They take care of themselves and deliver."

I was never to be promoted past my department. I built a team so valuable that I had also throttled growth for any of us; unless it was a new initiative that was going to require more work and problem solving than anyone would ever want. Then there were opportunities to work even harder for a few more dollars and a title change. It was extremely hard to get out of operations. We were just too good at what we did, and the existing leadership could sow doubt about our abilities to do anything else in a way that kept us from fighting for more. We just worked hard.

None of us had been off for Thanksgiving or Black Friday or that whole long weekend since we started our jobs. We worked in online shopping. We had thousands of merchant pages to optimize and protect. We had merchant relationships to respond to for our sales team. We had 10+ APIs loading massive volumes of affiliate coupon codes and offers to process. And sometimes we got a $50 gift card, an extra day off, or a company sponsored lunch for our hard work. We were the gold standard for "Set It and Forget It."

That is until one of two things happened. Either there was some kind of catastrophic breakdown in processes or we became too invested in a project that wasn't ours to own. One of the first crises we encountered happened on Cyber Monday after the team had worked two solid weeks without a day off. During Thanksgiving and the following weekend, the whole team worked every day including Thanksgiving Day and the following weekend. We also worked on the previous weekend to make sure we were ready for an influx in volume from our API feeds. We also needed to have hundreds of merchant pages optimized for the shopping holiday. Each team member doubled up on how many pages they could work. Everyone jumped in to help process thousands of extra data from the APIs. Six people would do the work of sixteen.

By Cyber Monday the team was tired, but we started at 5:30 AM that day. Unlike any preceding year, the APIs flooded our system with a crushing volume of work. We could work each piece of data at an average of one to two minutes apiece. There was no way we could keep up. We certainly couldn't optimize pages; much less catch any mistakes that appeared on them. As we fell behind, the Paid Marketing VP stormed into the department demanding to know why a particular merchant page wasn't perfect. I don't even think it was a merchant that would make the big money. Then our own VP would charge over to demand to know why we were falling apart. Volume. We couldn't handle the unprecedented volume, and I was wracking my brain to find out why I had missed any warnings about volume.

It wasn't me and it wasn't my team. It was simply the first year that the companies using the APIs held onto their Cyber Monday deals until the morning of Cyber Monday. But the stress was unbearable. I was right there with my team working as fast and hard as I could. I finally barked at the Paid Merchandising VP to please leave. He wasn't helping us fix the problem. Once the day was done, sales goals had been met, and I honestly felt like a dog that was the target of frustration. By the next year, I would definitely have a plan to mitigate the expected flow of volume. But in the immediate aftermath, my job was to lift up my team and make sure they understood they did nothing wrong. They did the best they could to get through a stressful day as a team and it was that kind of teamwork that made them special and more valuable than any senior leader would ever know. When tangible rewards are minimal, it's a leader's job to amplify self-esteem across the team.

We proved we could learn from challenges to create operational efficiencies in even the most stressful of times. We never experienced another Cyber Monday like the one that should have broken us. I communicated the problem and the solution to senior leadership, and then we made sure, as a team, that we had the right solution. In the coming years, we also added an offshore team of 50 workers. This would create new work and challenges as the team took on the creation of technical instructions for people in India.

Where offshore teams are touted as a solution for overworked teams, they are a tradeoff. They require active management, instruction, data analysis and cost savings reports. They require constant oversight in order to ensure they keep up with volume and quality of work. Our offshore processes began in the Product department, but soon became a part of our team because… we took care of ourselves and delivered.

As the new corporation took over and began to integrate with our company, there was never a doubt that the same 6 people could take on another 4 websites and their operating systems. Sadly, we could do that. Again. Work ethic throttled the obvious. There was opportunity for growth from high performers. But why? Set it and forget it. It would take a few years before a new leadership position was created. The company finally agreed that an offshore manager was needed. The company did not agree that the new manager needed her own team to support an expanding offshore operation. She was on her own. We could have easily been crushed under the weight of the work, but we always managed to succeed at the expense of our own career growth and self-esteem.

At this point, it was my responsibility to stand up for my team. I would need to be the advocate for their career growth. I would need to slam my head hard on that glass ceiling. Y'all. That thing is made of polycarbonate. It does not break.

Premise: Hard work is no guarantee.

Leadership Lesson: It's important to adapt to a changing workforce. If you can do that, you can build trust and loyalty in even the most unfamiliar settings.

The Last Place on Earth

"Hello, Michael. Why do you come home now?"
"Hello, Mother. Seems I've come crashing down."
"And you come here for help?"
Joanna stood rigid, peering out with steely eyes from beneath that old sun bonnet she had worn since girlhood. Her mouth was set firm with years of hardship and scraping to get by. She didn't look the least bit happy to see her son.

Michael lowered his head like a scolded child and drew little swirls in the barnyard dirt with the toe of his Cole Hahn loafer. He was afraid to look up. He knew she was glaring at him with no hint of love or happiness for his prodigal return. Her little border collie stood alert by her side. He knew that dog. It was a mean little mongrel known to bite anyone it sensed displeased Joanna. Michael hated the place, really. It was the last place on earth he ever wanted to be. The smell of cow manure surrounded the old barn that had been patched together for seventy-five years by generations of the Smidovec family. The cows gathered around it waiting for Joanna's daily delivery of sweet feed. Today she was holding a dirty old feeding bucket on her right arm. He knew it was filled with yard eggs. She was making her morning breakfast.

Michael dared to lift his head just a little. He could see that she was in her stocking feet. He knew her thinking. "No need wasting the soles on a good pair of shoes." She only had two pairs. One for mass and one for the occasional trip to town. All in all, she was a practical woman wearing practical clothes, living a practical life.

Michael, on the other hand, had run away fast after high school graduation. He had hustled and lied his way through college and on to a cushy job in Dallas. He spent every dime he ever made. After all, a man like him would always be in the cash. He forgot about his widowed mother. He rarely came to see her. For him, she was an embarrassment. The tiny crack in his well-designed lies. How would he even begin to explain the truth to his associates and so-called friends? Why did Smidovec become Smith? Was it to make his name convenient to those who met him or was he just that ashamed of his simple, impoverished upbringing.

"Michael, I crash every day. I have nothing for you." Joanna was the first to speak.
"I'm your only son..."
"Michael, go away. It is too late for you here."
A frolicking calf caught the dog's attention, and it ran off barking excitedly.

Michael felt a pang of hunger in his stomach. He suddenly longed for the warmth of a rough quilt that he could hide under in that old feather bed. There was no more high thread count sheets in a high rise condo. His girlfriend had dumped him for his business partner. The bank had frozen his account, and people had stopped calling. He had not been Uptown in a month. He couldn't even afford a drink there. He waited for Joanna to invite him in. She walked past him without a word. He decided to take that as a positive gesture, on her part, and followed her into the little farmhouse. He sat at the small Formica table that had been in the kitchen since long before he was born. Joanna continued her morning business as if he didn't exist. She placed her eggs in a waiting bowl, put her bucket beside the back door, and walked to the sink to wash her hands and a few coffee cups that had gathered there. As she busied herself with breakfast, Michael thumbed through church bulletins, a few local papers and little notes Joanna had made for herself.

One note in particular caught his eye.
"See Mr. King about the lease."
"Mama, you got oil on this place?" Michael could feel the excitement bubbling in his mind.
"That ain't none of your business," she snapped.

Michael wondered if Joanna had a will. He figured she would have left everything to the church if she did.

"Mama, you want me to go to this meeting with the lawyer with you?" He tried to sound as caring and honest as he could.
"No."
"You already been?"
She didn't answer.

A few minutes passed in silence. Finally, Joanna set a steaming plate of eggs and two pieces of toast in front of Michael. How long had it been since he had fresh eggs and toast from homemade bread? He felt himself soften just a little. Without hesitation, he began to devour the breakfast. Joanna joined him a few minutes later. She began to say grace silently. He paused, put down his fork and crossed himself. They ate in silence. As he mopped the last yolk from his plate, Joanna stood up and began to clean.

"Your room is clean and ready if you want to sleep. Frankly, you look like shit." There was not an ounce of warmth in her voice, but that wasn't unusual. The fact that she was opening her home to him was monumental. He took her invitation and made his way to his old room. He sank into the soft old mattress as he sat to take off his shoes. His clothes were such a contrast to the simple, country room he had grown up in. They looked like uninvited guests. He looked towards his old closet to see if his old boots were there. They were neatly lined up with an old pair of sneakers, his Sunday shoes and a crate full of Wrangler jeans. She hadn't changed one thing since he'd left. He looked over his shoulder at the bed. The quilt was turned down as if she had been waiting for him. Without hesitation, he slipped between the covers and fell asleep as quickly as he had as a young farm boy. He slept for hours.

The excited barking of the dog woke him abruptly from his slumber. The sun was beaming through his window, and he was soaked in sweat. The stale taste of coffee assaulted his breath. He sat up and looked out the window. His mother was kneeling with one of her cows. The animal was calving, and she was helping it. Michael figured it was a young heifer. It was his mother's way of helping the young ones with their first birth. Had she only been as nurturing with her son. She never helped him with anything. He struggled through school. He struggled with acne. He struggled to make friends. No matter how hard he tried to please her, he never could. It was only expected that he would bolt the day he graduated from high school.

News from home was of no interest to him. He wasn't particularly moved when his uncle called to tell him that his father died. He even managed to miss the funeral. That had been the last straw for his mother. Without her husband, she had no income except what she could eek out of the farm. He knew she struggled. Amazingly, she managed to hang onto everything. In the back of Michael's mind, it would easily all be his one day. However, over the years, that seemed less and less likely. It was just a delusional dream.

As he walked down the hall to the kitchen, he could smell a pot of beans cooking. He could already taste them. He knew she served them with steaming hot homemade cornbread. He couldn't wait. He took his place at the table again. He knew he should go outside and see if his mother needed his help with the calf. He just didn't feel like it. It was such a lowly way to live, and even if he was broke and disgraced, he didn't want to retreat to being a farm boy again. He got up and poured himself a glass of iced tea. He looked out the kitchen window to see his mother walking across the barnyard. She was soiled with mud and blood. Yet there was a peaceful expression on her face. Truly. She loved this little farm. She came into the house, and without acknowledging Michael, she began to wash up. He stood there, beside her at the sink, and made a point of not moving. He would force her to look at him. Why he thought he could outlast her was a ridiculous mystery. She finished cleaning and walked out of the kitchen as if she were in the house alone.

Dinner came and went. Not a word was said between them. It went on this way for two weeks. Michael couldn't believe he wasn't going insane, being so disconnected from his city, his associates and his life. Just sleeping, sitting in silence and reflecting on an invisible future were more comforting than any big dollar deal he had ever swindled out of anyone. On the first day of the third week of his uninvited stay, Michael got up and walked to his closet. He pulled a pair of jeans out of the crate. To his surprise, they still fit. He had certainly done his best to feed his vanity by going to the gym daily, but the fact that a twenty-year-old pair of jeans fit seemed to be a divine sign. Without hesitation, he threw on a t-shirt and his old boots and headed straight out to the barnyard. The sun was just cresting the horizon. He wasn't even sure if Joanna was awake yet. His hope was to surprise her with a bucket full of eggs. As he entered the barn, the chickens began to cluck and growl.

"Good morning girls. What ya got for me?"

"Bucket's behind you."
He was startled by her voice. She was standing there in her bonnet and stocking feet. The dog was at her side. She stared that intense gaze. There was not even the hint of a smile on her face.

Farm life was a cycle. It was born and then it died, but the farm never failed.

"Welcome home." She turned and left the barn. He could see her heading for the field to check on her latest calf arrival.

Chapter 9
It's Like a Bad Marriage

Here's the crazy question.

Why do we stick around and accept a dim outlook on our careers? What is that all about?

I had the executive assistant say this to me one morning over coffee…

"It's like a bad marriage. You're not happy, but you've got too much invested in it to leave."

Honestly. That's the best analogy of women and work I've ever heard. Regardless of all the advances we've made towards gender equality, it's not equal. I started my career in tech in my mid 40s. I was well beyond naive thinking. I knew where the bullshit came from, but I also needed to make a living, and I was already old enough to think I didn't have the flexibility to move around the industry. So, I stuck it out. I worked and managed my team for an embarrassingly low salary. In fact, the entire team worked for a slim income. We weren't going to get what we should have been earning, so I set my mind to making the time we had together as good as possible.

I built a layer of insulation around my team. I stood up for them. I was honest. I fought for their value. I was honest about my failures to get them what they deserved. In exchange, I was the shit umbrella. I was the sympathetic ear. I was the cheerleader. The boss who used every idea I could find to make up for poor pay. And that team was loyal. I hired people smarter than me, and I listened to their ideas and recommendations. We tried those ideas. Most worked. I let them own their department. And after about 8 years of leading them, I finally stepped back and let them be the experts. I made my job about championing them.

It was probably a selfless mistake, but I gave them their credit where it was due. I noticed most of my male counterparts didn't do that. A few did, but most gave no credit during meetings. They stated the win, but not the winner. My approach made me respected as a manager, and loved by my team, but at the same time, it was a good reason to overlook me. So, I got comfortable where I was and decided I could hang in there until retirement.

However, as the years moved on, I became more outspoken about bad directives. If "director" was as far as I was going, then I'd be directive and blunt. I would speak about the complexity of my operations team's tasks. I would fearlessly dive into new and messy platform acquisitions. And I would learn that not everyone has my ability to withstand stress and constant context switching. And certainly, the team was tired of the low pay and low recognition.

Another Brief Interlude

Let your best birds fly.
Open the door to the cage and let them go.

What does that mean?

I always told my team that I would support their life goals. I wanted them to become the very best they could be, so if they moved to a better position or moved to a better company, they would go with my blessing. I wouldn't horde them. In return, I knew I was getting the best work possible from the best people. I would help them and support their education and initiatives to beef up their skill sets. I'd pitch for them if they were ready to move into product management roles, or sales roles, or engineering. I would give them a good recommendation if they took a job elsewhere.

What I got in return was the best of people. Their best work, their best spirit, their best loyalty to the team.

What I was responsible for was burnout for some, fear of leaving for others, gratitude from a few.

This is all to say that we can sometimes push too hard as leaders. It's good to do that until it's not, so it's very important to know where the kill switch is. As workers were pushed to their highest potential, other departments caught on and piled on the expectations and work.

"Don't worry about her and her team. They take care of themselves and deliver."

Low income. Higher than average expectations.

As a leader, learn to say "no."

I taught my team to do this when cross functional teams asked them to take on new tasks that bordered on tossing a hot potato: Ask what the material impact of the ask is. If that question can't be answered to corporate satisfaction, the answer is "No. We can't do that for you."

When the inflow of big and complicated tasks continued to pour into the department, some of my best people left. I take responsibility for that. Those that left for their mental health and personal wellbeing v. those that found better jobs.

Workers find better jobs. Managers run them off. Two different things, and no manager is guilt free of running good people off.

Take responsibility for your decisions and actions; good or bad.

Premise: Championing a strong work ethic leads to burnout.

Leadership Lesson: Hard work is important, but make sure to measure the outcomes. When money isn't available, measurable outcomes that tell a success story can give a tired team a boost.

Chapter 10
Don't Expect People to Share Your Dreams

Many years ago, I went to a convention for hospice workers. I attended a session on culture. After all, hospice workers encounter all kinds of people, religions, stories, and death rituals. The more I knew about how to honor patients and families in their most intimate time, the better I would be at inspiring the communities my organization served to support our work.

The presenter said something that I thought was groundbreaking. She said that each individual is a unique culture. No two people believe and move through the world exactly the same. Certainly, culture grows into something bigger than one person as history, rituals, religion, geography, food, love and war shape a place, but even the culture of the place has microsystems that differ.

Movements arise out of shared ideas and desires. But if you're expecting your passion to be everyone else's, think again. In general, people may like what you have to say, but that doesn't mean they're ready to throw in their wholehearted support, work and money.

The DEI movement fizzled as fast as it materialized in the corporate psyche. Granted, the company I was working for has held onto the effort, but it's really not much more than lip service. Earlier I referred to the Hispanic ERG's corporate presentation on Hispanic Purchasing Power, and as of my termination a year later, the corporation had not shown support for digging into the initiative to open the Hispanic market to company publications and websites.

At the corporate level in New York, no one in the C-suites made the directive to the various business units to encourage and engage in DEI and outreach to consumer markets that matched our internal DEI efforts. The various ERGs had big dreams, but the company didn't really share them.

I think ERGs are important, even if the corporate objectives relegate them to social groups. Within each resource group, the members do good for their communities. They raise money. They mentor. They engage. The ERG members are the corporation, and for the company, that is good enough. But it feels limiting. Social governance reports will include bar charts and statistics around hiring diversity and leadership diversity, and if a low percentage from last year moves up even one point this year, that's a corporate victory. But honestly. It's posturing. It's not impactful.

A good leader sees people. A good leader remembers where they came from. And a good leader can imagine the struggle for someone who doesn't fit the corporate mold of privileged, white or male. So, a good leader must mentor and champion the rest of us. Most in leadership positions would say that's hard to do. They're busy. They have goals to achieve and meetings to attend. I know for sure, it's easier than they want to admit.

As a director in my business unit, I was in a leadership position for an ERG. I also attended events and meetings for the other ERGs. People across the entire global corporation knew me as an ally. As someone who saw people. Who cared about people. Who celebrated people. If I did nothing else, I did my best to make people feel seen.

With that I would say that if you're still reading and haven't given up on me, you know that I'm presenting a very different model of leadership. It's one that doesn't include executives. It's one that is achievable by anyone. Anyone who wants to champion their co-workers can be a leader. I can't bust that glass ceiling, and I think that's probably o.k. I've done more from underneath it than I would have on top of it in a corporate setting.

However, I do have the opportunity to step around it on my own. But again, my dreams are mine, and to expect others to fall in step with me is naive. I must look back at the times I drove my team to work too hard and say "yes" too many times. People are tired. They're as tired as I am. Most people are not looking for extracurricular work on my feel-good aspirations.

What my team wanted more than anything was for others to do their part. I did too, but I also knew that many people in a corporate setting are in over their heads. They may say they're an expert while throwing around overused corporate catchphrases, but most will never make the effort to learn and execute on anything they aren't directly instructed to take on. And senior leaders who don't understand a process will definitely grab onto cliches while dumping more on the team they trust to keep their personal reputation intact.

I think corporate ducking and hiding is not unique to corporations. It's the way of the world when it comes to new initiatives and the work they create. People will cheer you on, but to expect them to roll up their sleeves and pitch in on a movement is naive.

That means a leader must do the groundwork. The research, the business plan, the financials, the launch.

Leadership is hard work.

I get these big ideas that fill my heart with compassion and excitement, and when I share my enthusiasm, I very quickly learn that it's *my* idea. If I really want to see it grow, it's up to me. If I can get it off the ground, and people start to notice, it's time to pitch it again. Doesn't mean people want to work on it with me, but they may be my future audience or "customer". What is more important is to let that idea simmer. I often find that I care much less in a week.

We all get these bursts of passion. We must be careful about acting on them before we've let the feeling settle. A really good idea will linger, and if you give it the space to develop, you may find you're onto something amazing. Time is my enemy on most days. I want to move fast. I want to whip up the goodness immediately. I think I'll run out of time. It's simply not true. It's ok to take my time.

As I slide into my 60th birthday, I still struggle with speed. Speed was a mental problem in the workplace, too. It was an asset most of the time because I could attack a problem with velocity. However, it was an Achilles heel, too. On one foot, speed was expected; especially from leadership that had no idea what it took to complete a task. On the other foot, a little patience and slowing of the pace was ok. Velocity can be very stressful. Not everyone deals with it well, so understand that it's ok if there are team members who move a little slower, with a little more intention. A good team has a mix of sprinters and marathoners. They balance each other with nudges and tugs.

One thing I definitely learned about corporate leadership was this. If a boss came at me with velocity and anxiety about why my team or I hadn't already done something we didn't either know about or prioritize, there was a very good chance that his boss had put him on the spot. Maybe not with a question about why something wasn't done yet, but probably a question that required knowledge and understanding of my boss' department, and he couldn't answer it. When the boss felt dumb, he headed to my backyard to find a dog to blame. This is the very most exhausting part of leading from the middle. This is where I had to pull out the shit umbrella and hold it steady. It required a calm demeanor. A level head. A steady tone. And a balance of empathy and assurance. Of course, it usually required a low key way of educating someone who didn't bother to learn beforehand. An approach that didn't make him feel stupid.

You have no idea how much I hated these situations. There's nothing like a lashing while sewing up the wound.

Much like my dreams, I couldn't expect people to understand why I moved so fast, or why I was so checked out at the end of the workday. Even so, it's up to the middle leader to lead the way.

Fact: The executive assistant is the middle leader. The real force behind the company. I just wanted to say that. Executive assistants run the corporations from day to day. A great CEO probably has an amazing executive assistant and chief of staff.

Premise: Big dreams have a small audience.

Leadership Lesson: Don't be afraid to fail. You are the cheerleader in chief, but sometimes the team just isn't buying it. Assess your mission. Make sure you didn't create it in your own echo chamber. It's not necessarily a bad mission, but it may require some serious edits.

Chapter 11
Tectonic Shifts

As I write this little book, the tech world is shifting… and not just a little bit. AI has stormed the building. Nobody was ready for it. Everybody talked about it like an old friend, but the truth was pretty brutal. No one knew what to do with it. Sure. In small corners it was flourishing. ChatGPT is a comfortable part of our language. AI answers the questions we ask Google. Robots have been programmed to do human things for years, but as of 2024, it's not a maybe. It's an expectation that AI will take over the menial jobs. The basic stuff. The rote actions. The work an operations team like mine was doing.

Business owners are scrambling. Corporations are dumping staff. Efficiency is the reward as AI comes to town. As I mentioned earlier, I am not technical. I don't code. I can fumble through HTML. I can learn systems. I cannot design or lead a product launch. I am squarely the doer. The everyday problem solver. My early exit from a tech job didn't hurt my feelings. It came sooner than I planned, and *that* was an earthquake. However, it felt more like a trimmer. I'm ok with it. I really LIKE this easy, semi-retired way of being. Albeit it won't last forever because I will need to make some money for a few more years, but it feels really good to live at an easy and meaningful pace.

Me aside, what does it mean when AI comes for our jobs? Where will those that are affected go? What will they do? Especially if they aren't technical. My personal opinion is that the really big shift is the one that takes us back to pre-tech saturated days. Even before social media. I think AI's greatest gift will be the way it forces us to be face to face again.

Intimacy. Locking eyes instead of looking below the webcam at the image of a friend or lover. A handshake where we feel flesh and warmth. Where we measure a person by his or her grip.

Where we feel the sweat that tells us they are nervous and only human.

I do swear. My way of viewing the world is coming back into vogue. In the aftermath of a layoff, I have lunch with friends and associates. I lazily read the news. I read books. I sleep in. I am really excited to spend real time with real people. I literally have a bit of an aversion to Zoom or Google meets. I've stopped worrying about what people are doing all day. I don't follow Facebook with that minute-to-minute sense of urgency. I still don't use TikTok. I only look at Instagram if it's funny, and mostly when my wife sends me a video. I am perfectly happy to sit in silence next to a person and simply enjoy their presence.

Levi 501s and 505 are back on the bottoms of young people. Vinyl is cool. The mullet did what no one would ever believe it could do. It made a comeback (it's still ugly).

I don't know if this return to flesh and blood and breath has been going on for a while or not. Maybe I just got up from my corporate fall and finally noticed it.

As if the whole thing has come full circle, I am sitting in my office today arranging a meeting with a homeless man looking for help. He arrived in my hometown in search of a new beginning and I'm working to find the right resources to support his journey. I'm doing this with a group of childhood friends. They are the oldest and most stable friendships in my life because they've prevailed for a lifetime. Besides the texts and phone calls, it's a real time human encounter. This man needs people, not websites. And I am among a group of people who can and will help.

For all the time I lost to the corporate world, the cycle is back in my home territory. I think that is important. When it's all said and done, we all have the opportunity to land on the feet we were given.

A Final Interlude

If you want to lead people, get to know them in real time and space. Don't guess their height because that's what we do when we meet people online. Meet them in person. Save some money. Get on a plane. Meet your team. Meet your people. In a work situation, you will spend more time with your team than any other group of people, so if it is within your means, meet them in person.

Corporations don't like to pay for cross country meetups, but it matters. It creates an unbreakable bond. What does the C-suite get out of it? Stability and legacy knowledge. I think that's worth something. We're currently in an employer's market. The job seeker is not at an advantage. But this cycles. Right now, there's a right sizing in the tech world. Once it's settled, it is to every company's advantage to get human connection right. Don't pretend churn is ok. It's not. If the CEO isn't feeling it, the middle and below most definitely is. If the CEO doesn't care, that's a terrible human flaw.

I'll sit right here in the lap of humanity and enjoy it as long as I can. For those of you still toiling and excelling in your workplaces, don't be afraid to lead. Don't be afraid to be the person who lifts up the team or speaks up for the team. Leaders are in the company's departments. They're in the middle-class jobs or maybe even the poor working class. They are rarely in the C-suite.

Premise: The working class produces the best champions.

Leadership Lesson: Leaders never stop leading. Make sure to rest and take breaks, but know that you will be called to lead again.

Chapter 12
Practical Leadership Tips from the Middle

Hiring

The Cover Letter -

I find that one of the easiest ways to get a robust understanding of a candidate is via their cover letter. If a candidate doesn't provide a cover letter, I don't ignore them. I realize that some job search platforms make it easy to skip the letter, but I like to see one. I recommend that anyone applying for a job write one.

I want the letter to be specific to the job I'm promoting. It shows effort, and it shows that the candidate read the job description. A good cover letter will have details about the candidate's qualification for the specific job they're applying for.

I don't like cheesy sales pitches. I pay attention to grammar and spelling. I make sure the cover letter matches the resume qualifications, and if I decide to interview the candidate, I can usually tell from a real time conversation whether the candidate actually wrote that cover letter. That matters to me. I get it that some people prefer or need help with resumes and cover letters, but a bright and engaging cover letter should translate to a bright and engaging candidate. The syntax should match. This is to say, the cover letter becomes the source of truth. Candidates! Make sure it's honest and a reflection of you. Hiring managers! Make sure it matches the candidate and their qualifications. Cover letters take extra time. If someone puts in the time, put in the effort to review the resume closely.

For me, the cover letter is the first introduction into a candidate's personality. The first clue to whether they're a culture fit at my organization.

The Interview -

You should definitely have the standard questions ready, but I propose putting in a few questions unique to your team. I know HR professionals cringe at this, but ask things like, favorite book, favorite movie, favorite music/artist. Firstly, it can spark some casual conversation because you will want to know more about their favorites. This gives you some insight into their personality. Again, HR says it's a "no no," but it could also be the tie breaker with more than one qualified candidate. Will this person work well with your team if teamwork is required?

I never start an interview in a stiff, corporate manner. I always enter the room with a smile and a genuine welcome. I mix in a little small talk to loosen up the candidate and let them know working with me isn't something to stress about. I then give them a detailed introduction to the job description and ask if they have any questions before we move on. If while we're engaged in small talk, we actually create a conversation, I let that go for a bit because if you let people talk, they show themselves. As they loosen up, they're more likely to answer the "official" interview questions more honestly. In fact, they may willingly give an answer that disqualifies them. A relaxed candidate is an honest candidate.

I know not everyone is good at on-the-spot conversation. If you're bad at it, it's a good idea to ask someone who is good at it to pop in and introduce themselves and give a brief overview of working at your company. Get those candidates relaxed! If you hire them, they will eventually relax and be themselves. After the hire is not the time to realize you made a bad fit for your team.

The Team Expectation -

It's important to know what your team currently values in each other. Why do they gel or why some don't seem to get along outside of work-related activities. You probably don't want your team to be best friends (more on why in a bit**), but you also don't want disruptions because of personality clashes. Hopefully, you have a team of A+ individuals, and bringing on a new person is a breeze.

However, I have seen team fit ignored. I've seen company culture fit ignored, and the new hire didn't last. It is very hard to spend that much time with people you can't feel comfortable around. Know your team. If you hire someone who seems very different on the surface, make damn sure that perfect fit is under there. And let your team know that you are not hiring to make best friends, so not everyone on the team will be the same generation, belief systems, or gender. Build an inclusive team. Demand inclusivity from the team. If you start with that, then you really open the candidate pool in terms of unique and diverse individuals.

** Quick interlude on why team members who become best friends can be bad. Granted, most of the time, it's fine, but once in a while, it can be a disaster. If you have great team members who are good friends, it's unlikely their friendship will affect their work or the team. However, it can happen that friend "crushes" arise out of some subculture at the company. These "friends" tend to get into trouble together. It will happen outside of work hours. Usually over drinks and recreational drugs. I'm talking about the party set. In tech startup culture, the "play hard" adage is over baked. Beer fridges, happy hour Fridays, company happy hours with open bars, and then those infamous "after parties" are like a match in a box of dynamite. People can lose their sense of reason as they struggle to be in the "fun crowd." You may have noticed as a leader or as a team member that it's usually the fun crowd who shit talk the company. That's what people do when they're partying with workmates. It slides into company shit talk and gossip, and it will come to work on Monday morning. Watch out for this. Try to catch it at that happy hour. You'll hear the rumblings of the after party. You'll hear the whispers on Monday. You'll also hear the furious pounding of keyboards as the secret chat channels blow up with shit talking. This is toxic. It can ruin fantastic employees. I am not above bringing it up if I see it. I will do it in the spirit of protecting the team member from bad outcomes. I say something like this.

"I know you're good friends with xxxxxx. I know y'all have some beefs with the company. I know you gossip. I can't tell you what to do, but if you're going to shit talk, do it off campus. But mostly, don't do it. It never turns out well, and at some point, it goes to leadership over my head, and you are on your own."

It's also a good idea to have HR provide in-services on professional conduct and how even the things that happen away from work can affect employees at work. If an employee complains to HR about something that happened away from work while hanging out with workmates, do you know that IS the company's responsibility? So, if someone claims sexual harassment happened at a party on Saturday night, and they accuse a workmate, it is considered a fire-able offence for the accused.

Stop the toxic work relationships before they become poisonous. Do your team that favor.

Training

The SOP -

WRITE IT DOWN. Whether you call it a Standard Operating Procedures manual or a Process Documentation manual, put the effort into creating easy to follow instructions on every system and workflow in your department. Have the team experts for each process write the instructions. Then simplify the text, and use instructional graphics and pictures.

WikiHow is a good template to follow. It uses short sentences/instructions followed by a graphic. What you're going for is an "every person" document that anyone can follow. I used to say I wanted the team SOP to be my guide if I found myself alone having to do everyone's job. I should be able to follow those instructions and complete the task. New hires will learn so much faster with process documentation that is easy to follow.

The Teacher -

If not you, find the best teachers on your team. People who can explain concepts and workflows in simple language. People who are patient and willing to let the new hire try it themselves. People who are happy to answer any questions. And finally, you want trainers who check in on the new hire.

I personally believe that a good leader is a good teacher. A good leader makes the effort to understand the tasks within their department. Even if the leader isn't the trainer, the leader needs to demonstrate authority over the work. Some knowing of its value and necessity, and also, some willingness to do the task (with the instructions).

The Forgiveness -

People make mistakes. In the spirit of doing their jobs, mistakes should not be fodder for chastising, putting someone down or otherwise punching them in the morale.

I worked with a VP who would call people out for their mistakes in large meetings. He'd really shame them and put them on the spot. He may have held onto my response to those kinds of incidents and factored it into putting my name on the "lay off list." I'm not a fool. Guys like that are paranoid and have it out for anyone who disagrees with their leadership style.

But here's my response to him:
"If you have a problem with someone on my team because you think they haven't done their job, then send me a personal message during the meeting, and we can set up time to discuss the infraction. But never call them out and put them on the spot in a meeting. It is demoralizing and unprofessional. People make mistakes. They don't need to be publicly shamed. And if you don't understand something, please ask me before putting someone on the spot as if they haven't done the job as expected. My team has enough stress without that kind of hubris."

I pretty much knew that was the kiss of death. HR wouldn't address his behavior. They told me to do it. I did. I got laid off.

I don't think of it as punishment. I always said I would go down in flames before I allowed bully leadership to destroy my team's morale.

See your team as human. They will make mistakes. They may need a pep talk. You may need to understand what is driving poor performance. Ask questions. More than likely, you're going to find that there is something you can do to help their performance. Not everyone works the same.

I've had team members who get overwhelmed and need help blocking out their day to ensure they get all their tasks done. I've had team members who needed help recognizing when a cross functional team is pulling them off task to do something with little to no material impact - i.e. teaching the team member how to say "no" and empowering them to do so. And sometimes, there's something going on personally that is creating distractions. Give the team member a day or two off. We all need mental health days. Keep your team healthy. That includes their brains. And when you know it's personal, check in frequently. Ask how they feel. Ask if they need anything from you to better accomplish their job requirements.

Be kind. Go back to Chapter 2. Review "premise." X leads to Y. Now you should understand why I started with such an offbeat way of viewing the world.

Career Development

The Blue-Sky Dream -

In every candidate interview I ask this question.
"What do you want to be doing in ten years? What is your blue-sky dream?"
Then I make sure the candidate understands I want to hear the truth. I do not want to hear what they think I want to hear. I want to know them as a person, so give me the real answer.

This question has helped me make the right decision on hiring more than anything else. That blue sky dream tells me who they are and how hard they are willing to work to get to it.

As they settle into their work with me, I keep that dream in the back of my head. I look for tasks and opportunities that can help them build the experience to realize their dream. It adds value to their work, and not necessarily for the company, but for them. It often builds loyalty. When someone knows you see them for who they are, they become loyal and willing to ride the tough roads with you.

The blue-sky dream could be that place where new skill sets are developed, and promotions happen. Someone who dreams of writing satirical novels deserves the chance to write humor where it works for the company (I worked for a company that owned online magazines, so my writers got opportunities to write). Someone who is passionate about human justice and DEI can get involved in those company initiatives. I had a team member that I pitched as a perfect fit for the DEI team because that was her passion. I wasn't worried about losing a team member as much as I was about helping a young woman realize her dream.

Companies should be synergistic. Don't talent horde. If someone is a better fit in another department, advocate for them. And if someone realizes that blue sky dream, let them go with your blessings. You are a leader, so lead people towards their true path.

The Path from Here -

I have a blue-sky dream. I'm working on it right now. I am a writer, a creator, and student of human experience. I spent most of my working life doing what I had to do to survive in the practical world. Remember that your team members are likely doing the very same thing. Don't begrudge them.

Leadership is a culmination of experiences. Leaders win and leaders lose. Leaders make horrible mistakes, but they own up to them. Leaders never downplay the humanity of the people who work for them or follow them. It's a responsibility. If this isn't the kind of journey you want, don't lead. Please don't.

Your path is not one of promotions. It's a path that ends with a look back at your life where you see your success in others. If you don't have the energy or patience to stop and listen or take extra time to help someone improve at their job, or volunteer when you're needed, or speak the truth for those who rely on you, don't take this path.

In my mind, there is only one kind of leadership. Servant leadership. There is no power in it.

The Honest Promise -

Here it is: "If you find a job that you are really excited about, and you leave this one, you will leave with my blessing as long as you've been a good team member. I say this because as you grow into your dream job, I know that I am benefiting from your gained expertise, and I thank you. Use me as a reference."

That's it. Simple.
That is mentorship in action.

Mentorship is Leadership

This is where I challenge the mainstream corporate idea of leadership. I'll ask this: How does anyone lead if they spend their time with other C-Suite level people most of the time? Couldn't you say that anyone on that level is "there"?

Leadership is about guiding a team. A person. A student. A new hire. That means facetime. That means mentorship. Mentors guide, support, and listen. They get to know the mentee. That way the guidance is tailored to the individual. This takes time. It takes a level of empathy (never forget where you came from). It takes real investment. So, I propose that the real leaders are in the ranks. Team leads, trainers, managers, and maybe even directors. However, there eventually comes a promotion that makes it harder to mentor. It's not impossible, but often the executive leadership team perceives their time as used up on something besides the people who work under them. They may volunteer for monthly meetups with people seeking mentorship, but on a day-to-day basis, it's rare to get much more than that.

Leadership happens on the front lines. The kind of leadership I'm proposing is about the people, not the spreadsheet. It is an intense job that will challenge a leader's intellect and emotions. It takes practice. It takes commitment. It takes heart.

Leaders who are mentors don't require appointments that are made by an executive assistant; at least not beyond weekly or bi-weekly one on ones. It can and should happen during the workday. Ongoing engagement, training, working alongside and listening. I was once offered the hill country window view at an office I worked in because I was the manager and that was a perk. I refused it in order to sit in the center of my team's area. I told my

VP that I needed to support people on my left and my right. Sitting by a window would cut off one side. I needed to swivel and roll my chair around as I was summoned by my team. In fact, I was a working part of the team. No window view is needed but thank you.

Once those deep mentoring connections are formed, they should last years. They should last beyond the company that drew you together. Let friendship and trust hold your relationship together because it is hard to find good leaders, and a good leader doesn't walk away from a person that relies on their guidance.

Make a quick phone call or send a text. If you're genuine, then you're invested enough to do that. I keep a personal Slack community, and I invite people I've worked with, mentored, or admire and trust when I ask for help. It allows me to keep real time conversations and subjects of interest flowing. I can create group channels or simply send a message to an individual in the community. From my point of view, a leader doesn't quit, a leader slows down or finds a new career or retires, but unless there's a really good reason for it, a leader keeps a level of availability for those they have supported.

Passing the Baton:

Even though a good leader never completely disappears, they do slow down, retire, move on to other interests and career advances.

Communication with mentees, employees, team members and work associates changes and may become less frequent or it may become more of a casual friendship as work responsibilities dissolve. As the day comes to retire or move into a new phase in life and work, it's important to pass the baton. There should be people who can pick up your role and continue to support a team.

If we don't leave a protege, we don't leave a legacy.

The workplace changes daily. In corporations, the company you work for can look and feel very different than it did a year ago. Mergers, acquisitions, senior leadership turnover, layoffs, business direction, and team churn can change even large companies very quickly. Therefore, your good work can disappear very quickly.

In the training subsection of the chapter, I recommended an SOP or process documentation. That's a very good way to make sure your guidance is codified. There should be guidance on hiring, interviewing, training, job descriptions, and a promotion matrix that makes it easy to quantify staff promotions.

If people can see what steps and accomplishments are required to promote, they won't feel so lost or confused. They'll also have something to be accountable for.

Writing it down is great, but grooming your proteges is even better. Managers and team leaders should naturally be the proteges. Make sure you involve them in your decision process. Give them the responsibility of hiring, guiding, disciplining their team, but don't simply pass off the responsibility. Spend time teaching, suggesting, debriefing, encouraging. Don't take their individuality away from them, and praise their strengths, but do step up to assist when you're needed. Take your managers to lunch. Get to know them and understand them so that you can nurture their personality strengths into leadership traits. Make sure they know your point of view. Then make sure you communicate their ability to lead and give examples of why you think that. You're not only their mentor, but you are their cheerleader. And finally, once a person grows up and into a leader of their own, let them go to do *their* best, not your best. They'll come to you if they need you. No need to hover.

You plant the seeds of leadership throughout your life. It happens as you volunteer with underserved communities - as you inspire others. It happens as you tell your story; including the failures that helped you grow. It happens in the interview process with a new team member. It happens in the way you treat the store clerk or restaurant server. It happens when people see you stand up and stand out for the right reasons, even if you take a blow for doing it.

If you can't stand up and challenge the status quo, leadership will be hard because good leadership is underpinned by inspiration. I want to retire in a few years and feel good about the many people I inspired to be their very best and even more than that, their authentic selves

Epilogue

Leaders accept challenges. Leaders take on the work others won't. That work could be something strange and unfamiliar. It could be dirty. It could be boring. It could be an insurmountable volume, or it could look impossible. Failure is inevitable, but not fatal. Perseverance has to come from a superhuman strength within. Betrayal is a possibility. Ingratitude is waiting to pat anyone who tries to lead on the back. But a LEADER accepts the challenge. They commit. They are dogged in their determination. They won't always succeed, but they won't let one failure stop them.

Leadership challenges are everywhere. The person that steps up and takes the chance and the responsibility for change is the leader. The leader could be the mailroom clerk who spends their evenings and weekends building a support system for the homeless. A leader could be your elderly neighbor who bakes cookies for the neighborhood kids in exchange for a few minutes of their time in order to mentor and guide those children to dream. A leader could be the shift manager at McDonalds who recognizes the dark circles under an employee's eyes and spends break time with that person to find out how they can help.

The Leadership Premise goes something like this:
Commitment to something outside of yourself creates a leader.

Anyone can be a boss. Few rise to the challenge of leadership.

www.ingramcontent.com/pod-product-compliance
Lightning Source LLC
Chambersburg PA
CBHW071056240526
45471CB00016B/1942